First World War
and Army of Occupation
War Diary
France, Belgium and Germany

59 DIVISION
Divisional Troops
200 Machine Gun Company
14 April 1917 - 28 February 1918

WO95/3017/13

The Naval & Military Press Ltd
www.nmarchive.com
Published in association with The National Archives

Published by

The Naval & Military Press Ltd

Unit 10 Ridgewood Industrial Park,

Uckfield, East Sussex,

TN22 5QE England

Tel: +44 (0) 1825 749494

www.naval-military-press.com

www.nmarchive.com

This diary has been reprinted in facsimile from the original. Any imperfections are inevitably reproduced and the quality may fall short of modern type and cartographic standards.

© **Crown Copyright**
Images reproduced by permission of The National Archives, London, England, 2015.

Contents

Document type	Place/Title	Date From	Date To
Heading	WO95/3017/13		
Heading	59th Division 200th Machine Gun Coy. Apr 1917-1918 Feb		
War Diary	Havre	14/04/1917	17/04/1917
War Diary	Merigmolles	18/04/1917	18/04/1917
War Diary	Beaumetz	18/04/1917	25/04/1917
War Diary	Beaumetz	26/04/1917	26/04/1917
War Diary	Roisel	27/04/1917	01/05/1917
Heading	Zoo M.G Coy War Diary for Month of May/1917		
War Diary	Roisel	01/05/1917	04/05/1917
War Diary	Hervilly	05/05/1917	21/05/1917
War Diary	Beaumetz	22/05/1917	30/05/1917
Heading	200 Machine Gun Company 59th Division June		
War Diary	Beaumetz	01/06/1917	01/06/1917
War Diary	Etricourt	01/06/1917	23/06/1917
War Diary	Metz	24/06/1917	30/06/1917
Heading	Volume IV. July.1917. 200th Company. Machine Gun Corps.		
War Diary		01/07/1917	31/07/1917
Heading	Volume V. August. 1917. 200th Company. Machine Gun Corps.		
War Diary	Barastre	01/08/1917	24/08/1917
War Diary	Acheux	25/08/1917	31/09/1917
Heading	Volume VI. September. 1917. 200th Company Machine Gun Corps		
War Diary	Winnezeele	01/09/1917	19/09/1917
War Diary	Watou	20/09/1917	22/09/1917
War Diary	Ypres. N	23/09/1917	30/09/1917
Heading	200th Company, Machine Gun Corps. Volume VII October 1917.		
War Diary	Ypres N	01/10/1917	01/10/1917
War Diary	Steen Becque	02/10/1917	06/10/1917
War Diary	Petigny	07/10/1917	10/10/1917
War Diary	Marest	11/10/1917	11/10/1917
War Diary	Maisyilles Ruitz	12/10/1917	12/10/1917
War Diary	Chateau de la Haie	13/10/1917	13/10/1917
War Diary	Alberta Camp	14/10/1917	14/10/1917
War Diary	Odillion Camp	15/10/1917	15/10/1917
War Diary	Carency	16/10/1917	21/10/1917
War Diary	Lens	22/10/1917	31/10/1917
Heading	Volume VIII. November, 1917. 200th Company, Machine Gun Corps.		
War Diary	Lens	01/11/1917	06/11/1917
War Diary	Carency	07/11/1917	17/11/1917
War Diary	Tilloy-Les Hermaville	18/11/1917	19/11/1917
War Diary	Blaireville	20/11/1917	21/11/1917
War Diary	Courcelles Le Comte	22/11/1917	23/11/1917
War Diary	Equancourt	24/11/1917	29/11/1917
War Diary	Havrincourt Wood.	30/11/1917	30/11/1917

Heading	Volume IX December, 1917 200th Coy. Machine Gun Corps.		
War Diary	Havrincourt Wood.	01/12/1917	03/12/1917
War Diary	La Justice	04/12/1917	04/12/1917
War Diary	Havrincourt Wood	05/12/1917	05/12/1917
War Diary	Flesquieres	06/12/1917	10/12/1917
War Diary	Lechelle	11/12/1917	16/12/1917
War Diary	Flesquires	17/12/1917	23/12/1917
War Diary	Bertincourt	24/12/1917	24/12/1917
War Diary	Rocquigny	25/12/1917	25/12/1917
War Diary	Maizieres	26/12/1917	31/12/1917
Heading	Volume X January,1918. 200th Company, Machine Gun Corps		
War Diary	Maizieres	01/01/1918	30/01/1918
War Diary	Penin	31/01/1918	31/01/1918
Heading	Volume XI February,1918 200th Company, Machine Gun Corps		
War Diary	Penin	01/02/1918	07/02/1918
War Diary	Gouy En Artois	08/02/1918	08/02/1918
War Diary	Neuville Vitasse	09/02/1918	10/02/1918
War Diary	Durrow Camp	11/02/1918	19/02/1918
War Diary	St. Ledger	20/02/1918	28/02/1918

WO095
30174/13

59TH DIVISION

200TH MACHINE GUN COY.
APR 1917- ~~OCT 1918~~
1918 FEB

Army Form C. 2118.

WAR DIARY
or
INTELLIGENCE SUMMARY.
(Erase heading not required.)

Vol. I Sheet 1

200 M.G. Coy.

Instructions regarding War Diaries and Intelligence Summaries are contained in F. S. Regs., Part II. and the Staff Manual respectively. Title pages will be prepared in manuscript.

Place	Date	Hour	Summary of Events and Information	Remarks and references to Appendices
HAVRE	14/4/17	2/30 p.m.	Disentrained previous to No 1 Rest Camp arriving 4/30 p.m. Rations drawn. Company under canvas. Fine night. Posted Reported to Capt. Commandant. Strong wind.	J.S.G
"	15/4/17	—	Supply sufficient and Ordnance to complete. Arms & exercised. Instructions by O.C. and M.O. 2 men admitted Hospital. Company supplies. Heavy rain during morning. No extras (blankets) issued.	
"	16/4/17	—	Inspection of finistons by C.C. Orders received to move off 5/30 p.m. to Heatherne-at Point 3. Entrained 8/30 p.m. Company paraded at Colombard	J.S.G
"	17/4/17	2/30 a.m.	Left HAVRE 9/30 p.m.- 2nd 2 days rations drawn with men Ettr to water BOUCHY. Arrived MERIGNOLLES 2 p.m. proceeded to obtain detraining orders at 3/30 p.m. Very cold. Men billeted in hut.	J.S.G
MERIGNOLLES	18/4/17		Company paraded to march to BEAUMETZ. Halt for dinner at 12/30 at ESTREES crossed SOMME at BRIE at 3/30 p.a. arrived BEAUMETZ 6/30 p.m. Still raining. Company under cover.	J.S.G

T. Sempe Col. Swart
Copl.

WAR DIARY
OR
INTELLIGENCE SUMMARY.

Army Form C. 2118.

200 M.G. Coy

Vol I Sh. 1 & 2

Place	Date	Hour	Summary of Events and Information	Remarks and references to Appendices
BEAUMETZ	18/4/17	—	Co.Y & S.S — Rations drawn by Div Ration [?] to Div H.Q.	
BEAUMETZ	19/4/17		Cleaning up Coy. O.C. to Div ordo — 2/30 p. O.C. Adj. and Lt Moore proceeded to Reserve Bat. - Via FLECHIN. Coy. employed in digging Latrines, Refuse contains etc. —	T & P
BEAUMETZ	20/4/17		Reorganization of Coy. Lines having Bath S. for line of Saindeven. Cleaning up Coy. O.C. and Lieut Moore proceeded to front line position via BERNE and VENDELLES and so on to PIEUMEL WOOD returning to camp at 6/30 hrs.	S/34.
BEAUMETZ	21/4/17		Company training proceeded with in general machine gun work. H.Q. visited the lines occupied by the Company and expressed his entire satisfaction at the steps taken by the Company in Sanitation. The Town Major of the area also inspected the lines. O.C. paid a visit to H.Q. and received instruction regarding Administration Reports required. Weather — cold winds and clouds.	S/34
BEAUMETZ	22/4/17		Church Parade for Company 6-10/30 AM. Officers Men Ratios. kits, Iron Rations and feet inspected in the afternoon. Company employed generally cleaning up lines. B/2nd Cpl Hepburn proceeded to Divisional Gas School VRAIGNES.	
BEAUMETZ	23/4/17		Company employed on general machine gun training. In the afternoon Company practiced advancing with Harkin Guns and conforming with Infantry movements for open warfare. 16 Lieutenants visited BADGES at ESTEES EN CHAUSSEE. G.O.C. Division visited the lines.	

T. Seep's Col. Frank
Capt.

WAR DIARY or INTELLIGENCE SUMMARY

Army Form C. 2118.

200 M.G. Coy

Vol I sheet 3

Place	Date	Hour	Summary of Events and Information	Remarks and references to Appendices
BEAUMETZ	24/4/17		Company occupied in General Machine Gun training. 66194 Pte Grant was sent to hospital. The Adjutant I/Mid & I/M Out visited the first line position of Le YERGUIER via BERNES & VENDELLES — reporting at H.Q. 2/6th S. Staffs Battn H.Q. The Officers returned to Camp about 3 p.m.	
BEAUMETZ	25/4/17	1/30 p.m.	Company engaged in general M.G. work. Lectures and M/M Wild visited our first line position travelling via BERNES & LE VERGUIER. O.C. Actg No 1 & 2 Sections to support 178th Inf Bde in attack on their company with stein guns. Further work. F.C. It. Moore reconnoitred to 178th Inf Bde H.Q. at Roisel returning 6 p.m. Orders issued for moving up on following day to ROISEL	1/8/4
BEAUMETZ	26/4/17	9/45 a.m. 8/30 a.m.	O.C. & Moore & M/M Sutherland the Dinnesan & I/Cl Corbyn proceed in advance of half-company R & F.C. Corbyn proceed to BERONNE & Sutherland to CRAVIERS and attend convoy items. M/M Stern W/M Cpl Sutton & Sutton with 1 fighting limber 2 cock & 2 pack limber, heh No I & II Sections & M/M Cushen in detached for duty. Under M/M Lillington move to ROISEL. The detachment arrived It. No II Section & proceeded with the detachment arrived at ROISEL at 11.30 p.m. No I Section under Lt. Moore were to be taken up positions north of the Road at 4.30 p.m. M/M II Section Officers personally reconnoitred position & Junction at 9.30 p.m. I Section moved up to BEAUMETZ. Remainder of company remained at BEAU METZ	
ROISEL	27/4/17	3.35 a.m.	The 178th Infantry Brigade attacked the Germans enemy at L 5 D 18 ref France 62 c NE. the enemy rifles being found at L 6 0.5 to L 6 30. The final objective being L 6 c 55. No I Section were ordered to fix a machine gun barrage on	

J. Seafield-Grant, Capt

WAR DIARY or INTELLIGENCE SUMMARY

Army Form C. 2118.

200 M.G. Coy

VOL I
Sh. Nr 4

Place	Date	Hour	Summary of Events and Information	Remarks and references to Appendices
ROISEL	27/4/17	3.50	COLOGNE FARM. Zero hour being 3:55 A.M. and to left barrage seven minutes after zero hour. No II Section was ordered to put a watchful time barrage on MALAKOFF FARM and COLOGNE FARM, starting at zero and maintaining fire for the same period of 7 minutes moved. After lifting barrage both sections opened fire to maintain units with the most situation afforded normal again. The attack was only partially successful, the first objective being obtained. The Company developed no casualties. The remainder of the Company moved in BEAUMETZ and was employed in general Machine Gun training. Nos. 3 & 4 Section proceeded to ROISEL with rations and returned to camp at 5:30 p.m. Weather — cloudy but mild.	
ROISEL	28/4/17		Orders received at 10 A.M. for remaining left company to proceed to ROISEL. 2nd movement report at 11:30 A.M. and from BEAUMETZ and amount reinforcement of group being moved for the own water — company relief and reinforcement of group being moved forward to BROSSE No 3 Section under L/Sgt lefts ROISEL at 5 p.m. and proceeded to Company H.Q. No D., relaying 4 guns of No 175 Coy M.G.C. Relief was reported from its position at in Sunken road at 10 p.m. No I Section two guns of No II Section and situated at F.29 a 95 to F.29 a 95 and relieved in similar road running from 4.9 a 95 2 guns belonging to No 175 Coy M.G.C. situated in Sunken road. The retired party returned to 4.9 a 03. 3d relief was reported complete at 2 A.M. and the retired party returned (relieved) to Coy H.Q. at ROISEL at 2:30 A.M. No 4 Section under L/Sgt .... moved from ROISEL at 8:45 p.m. and proceeded at VILLERET and 1 gun of No 175 Coy M.G.C. and 2 guns Myr 2 Indian Div/y at VILLERET. The fourth gun relieving 1 gun of 175 Coy M.G. situated at L.7 a 95 in VILLERET. Relief reported complete at 2 A.M. Thirteenth party returning to Coy H.Q. at 1 A.M. All the above references refer to map FRANCE Sheet 62 c N.E.	

T. Seafsier Cronk
Capt.

WAR DIARY or INTELLIGENCE SUMMARY

Army Form C. 2118.

200 M.G. Coy

Vol I Sheet 5

Place	Date	Hour	Summary of Events and Information	Remarks and references to Appendices
ROISEL	29/4/17		No I, II, and IV Sections in the line with 16 June. No II Section on H.Q. in the QUARRY, No III H.Q. at BROSSEWOOD. No IV [H.Q. in] VILLERET. No IV Section VILLERET was heavily shelled during Apr and May Lt. Q.C. + Lt. Letcher.	App 4
		6/30 pm	Ration carts cannot now get up. A TEMPLE OX where they are transport & pack mules extra/infantry allowed at detrained H.Q. M/Lt C. DAVIES reported to division to strength of 7th Company.	
	30/4/17		WEATHER WARM summer DAY.	
			11.50 pm Orders received for relief and rearrangement of guns on following brigade — Orders issued for necessary preparations. The Secunderum Command occupies at 175 M G Coy.	
		A.M. 6/20	A. taken. As taken over positions and reconnoitred positions prior to relief and to front line positions in advance and with new's decisive defence rearrangement of guns in ascending portion of line. Taken over instructions received regarding portion of line to be taken over. The H.G. defence additionally followed by a line running E. and W. from the canals of L. 10. 1st Company, 100 Yds take over N. throughout the canals J.L. 10. position bounded by a line running E and W, dividing L. 16 and L. 22–23 and line running E and W, dividing L. 16 and 17. and L 22 = 23 position taken by M/Lt Davies and points out this positions The Second in Command taken by M/Lt Davies and points out their positions	
		9 Am	for the guns of No IV Section. A line of fire was cut out with new positions for front H.G. selected. All guns of the company retired and all withdrawn. The following orders were issued in regards to this relief and reorganisation of front.	
		11 Am	No I Section relieves on section by a Section of 178 M G Coy when relieves the Section	

T. Grey Col Tony
Capt

Army Form C. 2118.

WAR DIARY
or
INTELLIGENCE SUMMARY.
(Erase heading not required.)

209th M. G. Coy

Place	Date	Hour	Summary of Events and Information	Remarks and references to Appendices
ROISEL	20/1/17	9 p.m.	Arrived by train in billets at COISEL. 2 G.S. wagons sent to back-areas until further orders. **Personnel:** 2/Lt WITHERS will take over work at 9 p.m. at STACK DUMP. 2/Lt WITHINGTON will then be relieved 4 p.m. Transport NCO orderly and 2/Lt WHITNEY to be billeted at BROSSE until daybreak. Coms Fire guns from ammn column will be attached to No III Section for duty. Limber G.S. wagons to be reported to O.C. No III Section. No I Section and 2 pack mules will relieve the pack-mules with firing pty. WOPD and report to No II Section. 1 G.S. limber and 2 pack mules will take up return to No II Section. 2nd Lt Courtney to carry out orders.	
			ARTILLERY: not much firing but some at dawn. Gun trips and subsections sent out... will hand over the gun posts at the CHATEAU and No II Section to M.G.C. Lt No III will take up new position by No II Section at 5.30 a.m. & No 177 ty M.G.C. Do. No V will take up new position L 5 ptremot. Belgian 1st prenant at L 32 a 73 will relieve No 175 H 6 8q gun at L 16 B 75 a.73 The gun advanced at L 22 B55 will return 175 MAG. gun at L 21 6 a 75. The gun advanced in SUNKEN ROAD L 16. B73 will be relieved by 4 gun F 1123. Section... will hand over their position by L 16 a 93 The reserve gun at No II section will take up new position at L 122 a 81. The reserve gun of No II section with details of... of No II section at L 170 B 86 to No (4)	
			relay and details of No IV section for the first stage will be in support to No II Section also NoII Section will withdraw his extreme right flank muddy to down direction to NIZERZY and will assist those a... his guns and equipment... will be taken with the Sens guard & BROESE WOOD will be used resting equipment to accomp. the troops and returned H.Q. The gun will be relieved by No II Section, Sgt WARD at L17 A 55 bed with... Sgt WARD at L17 A 55 but & relieved by No II Section, Sgt WORD... tour to... Wilson trench & No IV S.A.A. gun	

T. Seagood Col, F. Smith

Army Form C. 2118.

200 M.G.Coy

WAR DIARY
or
INTELLIGENCE SUMMARY.
(Erase heading not required.)

No 57.
Sheet

Place	Date	Hour	Summary of Events and Information	Remarks and references to Appendices
ROISEL	8/9/17	9/pm	Guide officers will be provided by Sep Warr to guide route winners to VILLERET Reports re: No IV section, will report will all guns when base been completed. Group H.Q. will be established in COTE WOOD.	Msts
ROISEL	19/9/17	5:20AM	No. III and IV sections reorganisation of guns has reported complete to H.Q. 175th Inf. Bde at 5/30 A.M.	

T. Stafford-Grant
Capt

200 M.G. Coy
War Diary
month of
May/1917

Army Form C. 2118.

WAR DIARY
or
INTELLIGENCE SUMMARY.
(Erase heading not required.)

Vol II Sheet 1

Vol 2

Place	Date	Hour	Summary of Events and Information	Remarks and references to Appendices
ROISEL	1/5/17		39 mules, 3 horses and 9 bushers returned to permanent camp at BEAUMETZ owing to shelling of mule-lines. 2/Lieut DuBryer, Transport Officer to proceed in charge of camp at BEAUMETZ.	J.H.
		9/pm	2 guns of No 4 section at VILLERET relieved by 2 guns of No 175 m.g. Coy. Camp at ROISEL Shelled during afternoon and evening. Walker Fire.	
do	2/5/17	10/pm	Advance Head Quarters of Coy attached at HERVILLY, consisting of O.C., Adjutant and 14 O.R. Remainder of Company, into the exception of the 6 guns and necessary personnel in the line return to permanent camp at BEAUMETZ. 3.O.R. (reinforcements) report at 8/30 pm and taken onstrength.	J.S.W.
		5/pm	Situation Quiet. Hoses from 17 to 5 Bt.	
do	3/5/17	11/pm	Rle standing funding attack on MALAKOFF FARM. O.C. conducts to No 175 m.g coy and arranges dispositions of guns for attack. Necessary orders issued to OC Steele, OC. proceeds to the line. Zero 11/30pm. OC reviewing with No 4 Section relief. Completion of Operations, relieving m. troops 1 A.m. Walker Fire.	J.H.
do	4/5/17	9 Am	Situation Normal weather clear, day and hot. Receive orders to fire on some night lines 5/45pm. Enemy airman attacks our observation balloon and destroys it. The observer made descent by parachute landing near the Company conspect HERVILLY.	J.H.

WAR DIARY or INTELLIGENCE SUMMARY

Army Form C. 2118.

Vol II. Sheet 2

Place	Date	Hour	Summary of Events and Information	Remarks and references to Appendices
BERVILLY	5/5/17	7am	Situation reported Normal. Orders recd for internal relief. Relief was completed by 11.15pm. Where proceed to United Kingdom on leave for 10 days granted to specially urgent humane reasons. Operation Order No.2s cancelled 8.4pm. Heavy rain recd during night. Enemy shell in vicinity of gun position to E end of GRAND PRIEL WOOD. Detail H.Q. established in COTE WOOD. Gun fire during night 2000 rounds on Trench S. of COLOGNE FARM.	
do	6/5/17	7am	Situation reported Normal. O.C. visits permanent H.Q. at BEAUMETZ. Everything found satisfactory. Guns fired during night 1300 rounds on same night lines.	
do	7/5/17	7am	Situation reported Normal. Orders received to O.C. to report for Conference at Div H.Q. re the section in rest billets. Orders to keep these in readiness to see with No.177 Bde. Adjutant proceeds to H.Q. 177 M.G Coy to make arrangements (they are billeted close by). Orders issued for the necessary relief to Section Officers concerned. O.C. visits Line 9pm. Heavy rain and cold.	
do	8/5/17	7am	Situation reported Normal. Heavy rain during morning. Operation Order No.21 176 Inf Bde (received) do not effect the event. No firing by company guns.	
do	9/5/17	7am	Situation reported Normal. Orders recd for relief of No.177 M.G Coy from indefinitely cancelled. Orders received for O.C. to proceed to Div. H.Q. to Conference 5.10pm exceeded 3.45pm. Coy fire 2000 rds on trench S. of COLOGNE FARM.	
do	10/5/17	7am	Situation reported Normal.	

J.J. Hardy Lt.
O.C. Div.M.G. 200 M.G. Coy

WAR DIARY
or
INTELLIGENCE SUMMARY.

Army Form C. 2118.

Vol II Sheet 3

Place	Date	Hour	Summary of Events and Information	Remarks and references to Appendices
HERVILLY	10/5/17	10 pm	O.C. visits gun positions during morning. Guns are active during the day. Guns fire 1500 rounds on tracks S. of COLOGNE FARM.	9/14
do	11/5/17	7 am	Situation in line against normal. Little activity throughout the day. Weather extremely hot. Guns fire during night 2000 rounds at targets horses, M.G. emplacements at 6.13 & 8.6. (Ref. map. Sheet 62 c S.W.)	9/14
do	12/5/17	7 am	Situation reported normal. O.C. visits M.G. Coomp at BEAUMETZ and inspects detachments there. O.C. visits Bn. H.Q. re arrival of Divisional relief. Thirty guns during night fired 1200 rounds on dug outs & M.G. of COLOGNE FARM. Considerable work done on dug outs & M.G. emplacements.	9/14
do	13/5/17	7 am	Situation reports normal. Weather stormy and showers of rain. O.C. visits 176 Bde H.Q. in the morning and gun positions in the afternoon. All found satisfactory. Orders received regarding alternative M.G. emplacements. No firing has taken place no supplements carried on usual during the night.	9/15
do	14/5/17	7 am	Aeroplane bombs gun positions in the line. All satisfactory and work progressing. Little enemy rifle and gun activity. 2/30 pm fine following day. Weather fine with occasional showers.	9/14
do	15/5/17	7 am	Situation reported normal. Weather cloudy. 5pm Relieving party for the line leaves rest billets at BEAUMETZ. 8pm Relief of No F section	9/14

M. Harris O
COMDG No. 2

WAR DIARY
or
INTELLIGENCE SUMMARY

(Erase heading not required.)

Army Form C. 2118.

Vol VI
Sheet 4

Place	Date	Hour	Summary of Events and Information	Remarks and references to Appendices
HEAVILLY	15/5/17	8 pm	Commenced Relief reported complete at 10 pm. Adjutant in line during relief.	MH
do	16/5/17	7 am	Situation reported Normal. Very quiet day — Heavy rain during the day and greater part of evening.	MH
do	17/5/17	7 am	Situation reported Normal. Weather cloudy but no rain. A very quiet day. OC visits Bgs 173 & 174 Inf Bns H.Q. Adjutant visits BEAUMETZ – Everything very satisfactory.	MH
do	18/5/17	7 am	Situation Normal. Weather fine. Lively air activity. OC visits Gun position in line. Guns fire 250 rounds at hostile aircraft. Two O.R. leave ROISEL & attend 43rd M.G. Course at School, CAMISH.	MH
do	19/5/17	7 am	Situation Normal. Weather fine. OC visits M.G. Coy Camp at BEAUMETZ. Reports at Div. H.Q. Adjutant visits line.	MH
do	20/5/17	7 am	Situation Normal. Weather fine. Orders received that we are to proceed to BEAUMETZ and that 2 guns at L16.b.73 + L17.c.85 were to be relieved by No 174 M.G. Coy tonight. Necessary Operation Orders issued. Withdrawal & relief complete by 10 pm. Transport personnel & march to BEAUMETZ.	MH
do	21/5/17	12 mn	After party arrives at H.G. Camp BEAUMETZ. Weather rather heavy rain.	MH

J.M. Heaslip
Lt

Army Form C. 2118.

WAR DIARY
or
INTELLIGENCE SUMMARY
(Erase heading not required.)

Vol II/75
[Sw]/75

Instructions regarding War Diaries and Intelligence Summaries are contained in F. S. Regs., Part II. and the Staff Manual respectively. Title Pages will be prepared in manuscript.

Place	Date	Hour	Summary of Events and Information	Remarks and references to Appendices
HEAVILLY	21.5.19	10am	Arrived H.Q. and withdrew to R.E.A.V.1672. With removal camp etc by 3pm	JHK
BEAUMETZ	22.5.19	9.30am	Company employed in reorganization of equipment & kits. O.C. down to U.I.K.H. to procure furniture to HARDINGE room. Weather fine. Temporary command.	JHK
do	23.5.19		Company employ in general company work. M/Wilson who drew with programme just submitted to Division + O.C.	JHK
do	24.5.19		Rather fine. Company on Route march during morning + football match arranged for afternoon.	JHK
do	25/5/19	8pm	Tactical scheme all day - weather fine	JHK
do	26/5/19	8pm	Company goes for Route march for whole day. O.C. visits D.O. Planning orders to have new reward your order previous to release 2 anti-aircraft guns at NURLU. Os proceeds KNURLU to arrange with O.C. No. 218 Coy regarding relief	JHK
do	27/5/19	8pm	Necessary move to relief issued Copy despatched to No 218 H. Coy Church parade + Holy Communion - Afternoon football match.	JHK

J.M.Hardinge Lt.
COMDG. No. 200 M.G. Coy.

2449 Wt. W14957/M90 750,000 1/16 J.B.C. & A. Forms/C.2118/12.

WAR DIARY
or
INTELLIGENCE SUMMARY

Army Form C. 2118.

Vol II Sheet 6

Place	Date	Hour	Summary of Events and Information	Remarks and references to Appendices
BEHUMET	27/5/17	4 a.m.	No 5 & 6 guns returned to NURLU with 2/LT WHITE to return guns to No 2.18 Coy M.G.C. Orders received regarding general move of Coy. Company employed in preparation of move. Written route for Route march – No 5 Coy & No 6 Coy.	J.S.H.
do	29/5/17		During moving company to ESTREES – MONS – ESTREES – VRAIGNES. Afternoon General M.G. undertaken clean.	J.S.H.
do	30/5/17		Company in rest area. Parade during morning, company employed in General M.G. work. Afternoon gun cleaning Dismounted action & weapons taken fire – Operation orders for move issued. Transport officer proceeds to NURLU to arrange for extra transport for movt. 2/Lt WHITE reports.	J.S.H.
do	30/5/17		Company in rest area. Preparing for move. No hostile aircraft sighted.	J.S.H.

J.S. Hardinge

Army Form C. 2118.

WAR DIARY
or
INTELLIGENCE SUMMARY
(Erase heading not required.)

Vol 3

200 Machine Gun Company
9th Division

June

T. Stafford Smith
O.C.
Capt.
O.C. No. 200 M.G. Coy

WAR DIARY
or
INTELLIGENCE SUMMARY

(Erase heading not required.)

Army Form C. 2118.

Vol III (Sud)

Place	Date	Hour	Summary of Events and Information	Remarks and references to Appendices
BEAUMETZ	1/6/17	5 am	Company move to V.8.6. rd sheet 57c. SE via TINCOURT — TEMPLEUX-LA-FOSSE — NURLU to ETRICOURT, arriving at destination at 11/30 a.m. New camp erected.	JBH
ETRICOURT		12 noon	H.Q. established at V.8.6.14. Orders received to despatch 2 guns for anti-aircraft work at P.32.d. — 2/Lt DAVIES sent 6 reinforcements — Necessary orders issued — party despatched 6/30 pm — in position 8/45 pm. Lt EMSLIE leaves for U.K. on leave. (auth 100/53/113 - 30/5/15 AAA 59th Div.) Weather extremely hot.	JBH
do	2/6/17	7 am	O.C. & 2nd Lieut Davies proceed to P.32.d. to inspect A.A. guns. New position decided on for right gun — arrangements for general improvement of position. O.C. visits Div. H.Q. 3/25 pm. Weather very hot.	JBH
do	3/6/17	10 am	Church parade for company in camp. O.C. visits 2nd Lieut Davies for instructions regarding guns. Orders received to move guns to fire barrage. 2/Lt Moore returns from leave. Hostile aircraft active — gas alarm sounded at 11/30 pm — Gas respirators were put on + kept on for ½ hr. When orders were issued troops came in alert positions. Dismissed H.Q.	JBH
do	4/6/17	8 pm	O.C. Lt MOORE & STEELE visit 2nd Line Defences reconnoitre ground to be occupied by Ly + Capt Sit new M.G. emplacement.	JBH
		9/40 pm	Orders were regarding move. Courtesy baths + clean washing thrown clothing issued.	

T. St.[?] Lt Col Engrs Corps

WAR DIARY
or
INTELLIGENCE SUMMARY

Army Form C. 2118.

Vol VIII Sheet 2

Place	Date	Hour	Summary of Events and Information	Remarks and references to Appendices
ETRICOURT	5/6/17	9/am	No I Sn, No I Sec, Con 2 gun teams, No III Section has 2/4 Lewis & two 5 mm teams under Lt. HOORE went to METZ. Coy H.Q. remain at ETRICOURT. C.M.G.O. III Corps visits company and make arrangement regarding Anti-aircraft defer appliances — CAPT. J. SCAFIELD - GRANT H.Q. returns from leave and resumes command of the Company.	
do	6/6/17	9/am	O.C. & Adjutant visit 2nd LINE and inspect work being done on new emplacements returning to camp 3/40 pm. Situation very hot. Weather normal.	
		3/pm	A.A. guns at work. Anti-aircraft fire at R4.	
do	7/6/17	9/am	Schley ETRICOURT YTRES - fire on hostile aircraft — dropt the same off. 11/am O.C. visit Divisional H.Q. for orders — proceeds to 2nd LINE to see progress of work on emplacements. 12 m/h. Gas Alarm sounded - Men stand to & put on gas respirators — All clear at 11/AM.	
do	8/6/17		Situation normal. O.C. visits trench during A.M. during for intell. company adjut. O.C. visits CRE regarding construction of deep dug outs. Returns to camp 11/pm.	
do	9/6/17	9/am	Situation normal. No IV Section proceed to METZ at 8/5 am. Instructions of No III & II Section return to camp at P.32995 (Sheet 57c SE). Heavy thunderstorm during 11/pm. No IV Section return. No IV Section reliev No IV Section Anti-aircraft work at P.32995 (Sheet 57c SE). Heavy thunderstorm during 11/pm. O.C. visits works on 2nd Line Defences through ↔↔↔↔ & 256 R.E.Coy. in day wet.	
do	10/6/17		Situation normal. Church parade 10/am. Works proceeding progress in 2nd line. Set M.G. emplacements completed, 10 alternate emplacements under construction.	

J. Scafield. Emt. Capt.

WAR DIARY
or
INTELLIGENCE SUMMARY

(Erase heading not required.)

Army Form C. 2118.

Vol 5 sheet 3

Place	Date	Hour	Summary of Events and Information	Remarks and references to Appendices
ETRICOURT	10/6/17		O.C. visits A.A. guns at P.30 & 9r. O.C. with C.M.G.O. visits lines 9/10 Davies proceeds to Dublin to A.A. Ang - nm during night.	
do	11/6/17		Situation Normal. O.C. visits Div. H.Q. was a relief. Transport of Horse Transport moved to KHAVRINCOURT WOOD. a Transport for Dug-out construction	
do	12/6/17		Situation Normal. Construction of deep dug-outs for H.Q. employment commenced. Weather fine. Adj visits A.A. guns at NURLU. O.C. visits lines during evening.	
do	13/6/17		O.C. visits Div. H.Q. during forenoon. C.R.E.'s O. visits company.	
do	14/6/17		Very sat section of the E.R.E. experienced dep. depot 15 sections at rest engaged in instruction Base storing & hasting Entrens.	
do	15/6/17		O.C. visits B.G.C. & R.C.M.G.O. re A.A. Lt. section experiments depot depot to site R.E. Dep & please to O.C.L.12 24 Div. E.R.E. very quiet.	
do	16/6/17		Situation unchanged. Employment in dug-outs complete two to	

J.S. Gibb Capt

WAR DIARY
or
INTELLIGENCE SUMMARY

(Erase heading not required.)

Army Form C. 2118.

Place	Date	Hour	Summary of Events and Information	Remarks and references to Appendices
Etrucourt	16/6/17		Orders received to decentralise establish'd Coy HQ's. Necessary orders issued. Section north of Épehy in camp.	
do	17/6/17		O.C. visits lotting orders issued for 2 pdr Sect. to relieve 1st Coy H.Q. at 0.9.89 — 1st Sect. to R.E.d.f. Company balance to dug a.15.	
do	18/6/17		O.C. to de 2 withd [?] Tankelot — Valley — re 2 A.A. 2 gr 2 R.d. 2 nx hour to Coy H.Q. orders issued for Nº 1 are 174 Coy in Q.6.a.e.2 17 x 17 x & 22, 23 Sect. O.C. to H.Q. 176 Bde to reke and check coverey areas.	
do	19/6/17		Orders issued regarding relief. Adjutant visits Bde 174 Coy M.G.C. to arrange regu details operat. Coy engaged in miscellaneous operat.	

T. Seifert Mart [?]
Coy ? /-

WAR DIARY
or
INTELLIGENCE SUMMARY

(Erase heading not required.)

Army Form C. 2118.

Vol LIII
sheet 5

Place	Date	Hour	Summary of Events and Information	Remarks and references to Appendices
BRICOURT	30/6/17		O.C. visits Div. H.Q. to arrange for taking over new permanent camp site D.2.a.n.f. Heavy rain.	
do	1/7/17		Adjutant visits new Sector. Arranges with O.C. 174 Coy details regarding relief. O.C. visits G.H.Q.O. Rain during day.	
do	2/7/17		O.C. visits new Sector. Anti-aircraft fire at NURLU observed. - Relief complete 7/30 pm	
do	2/7/17 7pm		Coy moves to METZ. Coy relieves 174 H.Q. Coy commencing at 9pm. Relief complete at 11/15 am. No 3 Section, No 2 Section, No 4 Section & No 1 Section has 3 punkauers in line. No 1 Section has one pin & one Coy reserve. Rain intermittently during day.	
METZ	3/5/17		Situation Normal. O.O. visits front line guns. A considerable amount of enemy enquire organ positions. Enemies a.a. out of late firing. SAM enquire Ex.A. by Enemy quiet. peath. fires.	

T. Seafires. Cap.t-
Capt.

WAR DIARY or INTELLIGENCE SUMMARY

Army Form C. 2118.

Place	Date	Hour	Summary of Events and Information	Remarks and references to Appendices
METZ	25/6/17		AOI visits fire unit. Bde Maj 176 Bde Gp in. O.C visits Nos 3 & 4 sec/ns. O.C reports for R.E. work. Situation normal.	
"	26/6/17		AOI departed to IV Army School courses 27.6.17. Instructors 1.8.17. O.C visits No 2 sec/ns. LT Moore acting 2nd i/c arrangements made for M/Guy Coy H.Q to a point South of METZ — Coy HQM now G.20.d.1.4. LT. WHITE return from No IV School to entry O.C visits sections in turn. Situation unchanged. Weather showery.	
"	28/6/17		O.C visits Nos II & IV Sections in turn. Reconnaissance party found for R.E. work (150 R). Fatigue party (10 UR) to MIII Section. Duties unchanged.	
"	29/6/17		Visit from C.M.G.O. who visited sections with him. O.C. situation unchanged.	
"	30/6/17		O.C 15/17 Bde 16 Loncs reps. gun positions. Sit. during day normal. Under discussion further advanced reeces of tray Butts Wood also on edge U/S up Quarries of quarter i/c each except 5 Thickel 4 Sgt. Lock-outs. Instn: ongly to Notu of Guns, now french, each separately. Fired Lewis gun off. Reports.	
			Retention Men of Coy H.Q. refuged to Canton 29-30/6.

T. Sanders...? Capt.

Army Form C. 2118.

ORIGINAL COPY.
WAR DIARY
or
INTELLIGENCE SUMMARY
(Erase heading not required.)

Vol 4

VOLUME IV.
JULY, 1917.
200TH COMPANY, MACHINE GUN CORPS.

R. Mk. Lt. Gay.
CAPT.
COMDG. No. 200 M.G. COY.

Army Form C. 2118.

WAR DIARY
or
INTELLIGENCE SUMMARY

Vol IV Sheet-1 (Erase heading not required.)

Instructions regarding War Diaries and Intelligence Summaries are contained in F. S. Regs., Part II. and the Staff Manual respectively. Title Pages will be prepared in manuscript.

Place	Date	Hour	Summary of Events and Information	Remarks and references to Appendices
	1/7/17		Nos 2, 3, 4th Sections relieved by 1st Section Working Parties supplied G.R.E. Threatening enemy activity continues	
	2/7/17		O.C. wrote No 2 4th Section in the line, asking for arrangement made for concentration in night of 4.5.6. O.C. visits Bull Ring. 2/Command wired the 1 Section in the line. Working parties for Nos. 1, 4th Sections in enemy employment improvement & consolidation	
	3/7/17		H.Q. 6 function between General [?] & G.O.C. of "RAVINE" Trenches on front. O.C. met RE Major 2/4 Lincolns Working parties for No 1 & 4 Sections in their - completion of dug-outs + changing up trolleys to relieve in ranks	
	4/7/17		O.C. visits Bn H.Q. machine run A.A. position new Bn H.Qrs I.O.R. takes a sketch view [?] Portland stone Bull relieved in [?] in detail Next day & reports + [?] [?] Bunks	
	5/7/17		O.C. & Bn H.Q. & Div. N.Q. operations trench reconnaissance on night 7/6 Section detached & Work'y parties to Nos 1 H.Qs. Section in line + [?] new Sect. H.Qrs. Situation normal.	

2449 Wt. W14957/M90 750,000 1/16 J.B.C. & A. Forms/C.2118/12.

R Sherlock Capt [?]

WAR DIARY
or
INTELLIGENCE SUMMARY

Vol. 12
Sheet 2
(Erase heading not required.)

Army Form C. 2118.

Place	Date	Hour	Summary of Events and Information	Remarks and references to Appendices
	7/10		O.C. [illegible] Bn. [illegible] moved down [illegible]. Two new [illegible] counts [illegible] further down for [illegible] was [illegible] of [illegible] [illegible] [illegible] of 10/11th working parties to No 1 + 4 [illegible] St. Eloi Station [illegible] METZ ELLEN along 2nd ships from Coy H.Q.	
	8/10		Relieving Coy Commanders came to make arrangements for relief with their O.C. 8 Siege Co. to be relieved by 148 Coy. and 5 Siege Co. by 214 Coy. Instructions issued Pte's making move in early from billets of 148 Coy arrive to reconnoitre from [illegible] the [illegible] officers from 214 Coy. [illegible] [illegible] billets [illegible].	
	9/10		Advance parties 177 Coy to trenches when reconnaissance there is to take company accommodation where they arrive tonight [illegible] their after reconnaissance O.C. 214 Coy arrive with ample accommodation for same at O.C. 214 Coy arrive 2.30 pm with [illegible] and Major [illegible] agreeing relief at the Town Major's [illegible] [illegible] is not explained himself [illegible] unit cavalier [illegible] many important matters a [illegible] returned to his officers Sunday wrote orders [illegible] or 10 pm. No E.E. [illegible] No J. [illegible] 11.45 pm. Completed at 10.30 pm. 4th E.E. Section 10.45 pm 10 J. Section. All work back to camp marched by 177 Coy. officers in evident when the ones for men	R. [illegible] Lt. 9/10

WAR DIARY
or
INTELLIGENCE SUMMARY

Vol IV
Sheet 3.

Place	Date	Hour	Summary of Events and Information	Remarks and references to Appendices
	11/7/17		Return party under Lieut Bean paraded for Company on usual Parade 11.30 am. under 11.45. Intercompany athletic sports at night. Brunner, Company & Sergeants mess up win event. O.C. & Brunner. Prizes in cash distributed late.	
	12/7/17		O.C. visits Division. Practice firing on pushing trenches & training in anti-aircraft firing equipment. Weather very hot.	
	13/7/17		Lieut MOORE admitted to C.C.S. Inspection of company and guns by O.C. Football match versus 24th Bn Lincoln Regt in afternoon. Weather still very hot.	
	14/7/17		Limbers unloaded and sectional dumps made of gun equipment. Gun drill afterwards. Inspection and issue of clothing. Pay out in evening. Heavy rains during night.	
	15/7/17		Fire in morning. Church Parade arranged for whole of company. O.C. & 2nd in 2nd Lieut. MOORE. Running off heats for Divisional sports in afternoon. 2nd Lieut BRYCE leave to U.K.	
	16/7/17		Rain in morning. Guns cleaned and Gun drill during morning. Final football match for Divisional competition against Divl H.Q. won in evening. O.C. to Division.	

R. J. Vick Lt. O/C

Army Form C. 2118.

WAR DIARY
or
INTELLIGENCE SUMMARY

Vol IV
Chat 1-4
(Erase heading not required.)

Instructions regarding War Diaries and Intelligence Summaries are contained in F. S. Regs., Part II. and the Staff Manual respectively. Title Pages will be prepared in manuscript.

Place	Date	Hour	Summary of Events and Information	Remarks and references to Appendices
	17/1/17		Baths for all Company personnel in morning. Lieut VINT and 4 O.R. proceeded to attend course in Lewis Gun Recognition at 323 Squadron R.F.C. Hd a 5 run off with Divisional HdQrs in afternoon. Football match in evening v 174 M.S. Coy. Weather showery. Timbers wanted in morning. Football match played in evening against 2/1 South Staffs Regt. prior H.Q. won by scorer 1-1. O.C. 16 Division O.C. leave to U.K.	
	18/1/17			
	19/1/17		Parade consist of Gun Drill etc under sectional arrangements. 2/Cpls parade for communication will transport competitions in afternoon.	
	20/1/17		Parades as on 19th instant. Running heats for Divisional sports run off in afternoon. Arrangements made for all M.S. Companies to have range practice. Semi-final football match played in evening.	
	21/1/17		Holiday from 11/am for divisional sports which take place in afternoon. Very successful. Weather very hot. Transport & tending basket.	
	22/1/17		Church Parade arranged for whole of company in morning, and voluntary services in evening. Divisional Cup Final Football match in afternoon won by 3 goals to 2. Weather still very hot. Final arrangements made for firing on range on 29th instant.	
	23/1/17		Gun Drill, Semaphore and Range Cards in morning. Lance Corporals paraded for Communication Drill - Restriction in afternoon. Received Operation Orders for Divisional Tactical Scheme No 1.	

R. Mark Lt 6/17

Army Form C. 2118.

WAR DIARY
or
INTELLIGENCE SUMMARY

Vol V
Thur S

(Erase heading not required.)

Instructions regarding War Diaries and Intelligence Summaries are contained in F. S. Regs., Part II. and the Staff Manual respectively. Title Pages will be prepared in manuscript.

Place	Date	Hour	Summary of Events and Information	Remarks and references to Appendices
	24/7/17		Physical Training in morning, then Route march through HAPLINCOURT, YLU, and BERTINCOURT, then very hot. Company football match in afternoon. Conference in evening of Adjutants and Quartermasters. Subject Clothing.	
	25/7/17		Lieut Smelie went to D.H.Q. and was appointed acting D.H.Q. Lieut Steele remaining to No. 4 M.G. Coy. Company did Rough Ground Drill and Lewis Gun practice.	
	26/7/17		Lieut Steele and Section Officers Reconnoitred Ground for Tactical Exercise in morning. Lieut Smelie to Div H.Q. M.Coy did Continued Drill and Range buds. Secret Order received to send two guns to take over Anti-Aircraft positions from 2nd Australian Division at VIVIER MILL, near ALBERT. Lieut BRYCE returned from leave.	
	27/7/17		Company paraded at 4.30 am for Tactical Exercise. Guns in position 1/2 hr before Zero. Zero at 3.30 p.m. 2/B DAVIES and 2 guns and teams from No.3 Section left at 9 a.m. for VIVIER MILL on A.A. duties.	
	28/7/17		Company paraded for General machine gun work in the morning. Cpt. Karr proceeded to CAMIERS to attend No. 6 M.G. Course. Lieut. Glick admitted to 48 C.C.S. Two guns sent to 2nd D.S. for over hauling.	
	29/7/17		Church Parade in Camp. Heavy thunderstorm in the evening. Time off in the afternoon. 2 Lt. J. Thom + 2 O.R. proceeded to LEALVIE E R S to attend short course on machine Regulations.	
	30/7/17		Company paraded for general machine gun work. Weather uncertain. 2 Lt. C. White and 30 O.R. proceeded to VAL HEUREUX at 9 am to relieve 3 guns. No.3 Sec. McKelly C. proceeded to ALBERT to attend	

R E Watkins Kelly

Army Form C. 2118.

WAR DIARY
or
INTELLIGENCE SUMMARY

Vol IV
Year 6
(Erase heading not required.)

Place	Date	Hour	Summary of Events and Information	Remarks and references to Appendices
	30/7/17		A course at 7th Army Anti gas School. Company perused the sum of machine gun work (Regt formed Mounting) Auxiliary Mounting Drill, mechanism - S.a. + (Exemption) football match v. 177 M.G. Coy. Result, 2 no try 1 pant. 177. 2 points. Raining evening. O.C. visited div. tr. a.	
	31/7/17			

R. McK. Lt 7/11
CAPT.
COMDG. No. 200 M.G. COY.

Army Form C. 2118.

ORIGINAL

WAR DIARY
—or—
INTELLIGENCE SUMMARY

(Erase heading not required.)

Vol 5

Summary of Events and Information

VOLUME V.

AUGUST, 1917.

200TH COMPANY, MACHINE GUN CORPS.

W.Cruickie Lieut.
for O.C.

200TH COY. MACHINE GUN CORPS.

WAR DIARY
or
INTELLIGENCE SUMMARY

(Erase heading not required.)

Army Form C. 2118.

Vol V Sheet 1

Place	Date	Hour	Summary of Events and Information	Remarks and references to Appendices
BRAYASTRE	1/8/17		In rest camp. Divisional Tactical Exercise. Weather extremely wet.	
do	2/8/17		Heavy rain. Coy employed at "Mechanism" & "Stoppages" under cover.	1/8th
do	3/8/17		Divisional tactical ride for Officers during morning. Heavy rain in the a/n.	7/8th
do	4/8/17		Major Grant returns from leave & takes over. Coy employed in general M.G. Training. Commanding Officer inspects Coy.	
do	5/8/17		Sunday – Church parade in the Camp during forenoon. Heavy rain. Recreation during afternoon.	
do	6/8/17		Rain continuing. Section work with lectures on arrangements. Lecture on M.G. theory.	
do	7/8/17		Coy on box respn. All elementary practices fired. Capt Newcombe returns from leave.	
do	8/8/17		O.C. visits anti-aircraft detachment at DOULLENS & ALBERT. Remains O/N on general M.G. work. O.C. returns 9 p.m. Heavy rain.	
do	9/8/17		Coy employed under Sectional arrangements. 2/Lt White & Whittington appointed to command No I & II Section respectively in place of Lieuts STEELE & MOORE evacuated & struck off strength.	

W. Oswald Lieut
for O.C. 2ov M.G. Coy

WAR DIARY or INTELLIGENCE SUMMARY

Army Form C. 2118.

Place	Date	Hour	Summary of Events and Information	Remarks and references to Appendices
BARASTRE	10/8/17		Heavy rain. O.C. visit Division. Major Barton the D.M.G.O. visits the Coy. Employed at constructing M.G. emplacements.	
do	11/8/17		Coy moved to BEAULENCOURT & GUEUDECOURT to prepare emplacements & observation posts for long range firing following Hindon. Coy return to camp 2/30 pm. After dinner Recreation.	
do	12/8/17		Church parade – weather inclement – snow. Afternoon recreation.	
do	13/8/17		Coy proceed to old German line for long range indirect field firing practice. Raining slightly. 11/am conference held in this camp of all O.C. M.G. Coys in Division under D.M.G.O. Firing lasts till 7/30 pm. Coy returns to camp 9/30 pm.	
do	14/8/17		No 2 Section proceeded in motor lorry to relieve No 3 & 4 Sub-Section at DOULLENS & ALBERT. A Party proceed to M.G. Range to [?] O.P's from Ramsay Apollos.	
do	15/8/17		Pack Saddlery Drill in the morning. 1st Round of DIVISIONAL Boxing Competition. Weather fine.	
do	16/8/17		Divisional Battle activities. To Coy in the morning under Sectional arrangements.	W Brodie Lieut for O.C. No 17 Coy

WAR DIARY
or
INTELLIGENCE SUMMARY
(Erase heading not required.)

Army Form C. 2118.

VOL V
Sheet 3

Place	Date	Hour	Summary of Events and Information	Remarks and references to Appendices
BARASTRE	17/8/17		No 2 Sub Section at VIVIER MILL relieved by No 1 Motor Machine Gun Battery. Sub-section on way by H.Q. at 7.30 p.m.	
do	18/8/17		Pack Saddlery Drill & Laying of Guns for Barrage firing in the morning. Football match in afternoon. M/S Blackson's result ("Draw")	
do	19/8/17		Inspection of Company by C.O. in the morning, company & rifle drill under C.S.M. Lecture by Divisional Intelligence Officer at 10.30 a.m. on "The interpretation of Aeroplane photographs", all officers attending. Church Parade in the evening.	
do	20/8/17		Parade in usual Sectional arrangements. No 3 & Sub-section of No 2 proceeded to M.G. Range & Constructed Observation Posts for Divisional purpose. Weather very dull for such firing.	
do	21/8/17		Received Warning Division relieved & guns. Operation Orders issued for Company move off at 2.30 a.m. for the Tactical Scheme in 17B Range. Divisional & Brigade Staff's present.	
do	22/8/17		Copy of Memo received from D.M.S.O. The Divisional Commander has instructed me to inform you that he was very pleased with the S.O.S. first set up for the 6/1 you this afternoon.	

W Burchi, Lieut
for Major
Comdg. No. 200 M.G. Coy.

WAR DIARY
or
INTELLIGENCE SUMMARY

Army Form C. 2118.

VOL V
Sheet 4

Place	Date	Hour	Summary of Events and Information	Remarks and references to Appendices
BARASTRE	23/8/17		Cleaning of camp. Preparatory to move on 24/8/17. Capt Hotchkiss proceeded to CAMIERS for M.G. Course.	
do	24/8/17		Company left BARASTRE at 5-22 p.m. ACHEUX marched to BAPAUME & were conveyed to ACHEUX by Motor Lorries, arriving at new billets at 1/p.m. Transport & Lt BARASTRE 4-22 a.m. and reg ACHEUX 5-30 p.m. N°5 W. Section returned from VALHEUREUX.	
ACHEUX	25/8/17		Cleaning up & inspection of gun equipment. Lecture by Commanding Officer to Officers & N.C.O's on Barrage Fire. Weather fine.	
do	26/8/17		Church Parade. Officers rode in the afternoon weather fine, showers in the	
do	27/8/17		Washing Limbers in morning. Artificers fitting depression stops on Tripods. O.C. to conference at SENLIS 3 p.m. Very dull.	
do	28/8/17		Parade under Sectional arrangement. Lt Vint + 3 O.Rs. proceeded to WINNEZEELE as Advance Party. Weather boisterous.	
do	29/8/17		Very dull. received movement order. Parade. Company drill. Fitting sun shields on Q.F. Saddles. Issue of rations & water for move. Notification of postponement of move for 24 hours received 9-30 p.m.	

W. Hodge Lieut. F^M Ma^g
COMDG. N^O 200 M.G. COY

WAR DIARY
or
INTELLIGENCE SUMMARY

(Erase heading not required.)

Army Form C. 2118.

Vol V Sheet V

Place	Date	Hour	Summary of Events and Information	Remarks and references to Appendices
Acheux	30/9/17		Route march in the morning. Lecture by Section Officers to N.C.O's and No 1's on Barrage. Preparing for move. Weather fine but dull	
"	3/9/17		Company marched at 4-55 p.m. to BEAUCOURT via ACHONVILLERS, BEAUMONT - HAMEL arriving 7-40 p.m. commenced entraining at 8 p.m. completed 10-15 p.m. proceeded 11 p.m. to GODEWAERSVELDE arriving 11-30 a.m. 1/10/17	
WINNEZEELE	4/10/17		Detrained & marched 12-45 p.m. via market to WINNEZEELE arriving 2-30 p.m. Tents & Bivouac camps pitched 3-15 p.m. Weather fine. WR.	

W. Burnalee Lieut. / ?. Maj
COMDG. No. 200 M.G. COY.

Army Form C. 2118.

ORIGINAL
WAR DIARY
or
INTELLIGENCE SUMMARY
(Erase heading not required.)

Vol 6

Summary of Events and Information

VOLUME VI.

SEPTEMBER, 1917.

200TH COMPANY, MACHINE GUN CORPS.

W Dunketyfiew
for Major
O.C.
200TH COY. MACHINE GUN CORPS.

Instructions regarding War Diaries and Intelligence Summaries are contained in F. S. Regs., Part II. and the Staff Manual respectively. Title Pages will be prepared in manuscript.

Place	Date	Hour		Remarks and references to Appendices

2449 Wt. W14957/M90 750,000 1/16 J.B.C. & A. Forms/C.2118/12.

Army Form C. 2118.

WAR DIARY
or
INTELLIGENCE SUMMARY

Volume V Sheet I

(Erase heading not required.)

Instructions regarding War Diaries and Intelligence Summaries are contained in F. S. Regs., Part II and the Staff Manual respectively. Title Pages will be prepared in manuscript.

Place	Date	Hour	Summary of Events and Information	Remarks and references to Appendices
WINNEZEELE	1/9/17		Detrainment completed 12-45pm marched to WINNEZEELE arriving about 2.30pm Tents & ammn. dump pitched 3-15pm. Weather fine.	
do	2/9/17		Church Parades in morning & evening. Weather showery	
do	3/9/17		O.C. to YPRES with Corps Machine Gun Officer. Cleaning of guns & equipment	
do	4/9/17		Washing & rolling of linen. 2 men returned to M.G.C. Base as insufficient. No 1 section detailed for Anti-Aircraft duty in vicinity of WINNEZEELE. O.C. to YPRES. Weather fine.	
do	5/9/17		A.A. in positions allotted. Gun Drill with Box Respirators. Weather fine	
do	6/9/17		O.C. Section Officers, Section Sgts. & No 1 S. proceed to XIX Corps to see recorded of YPRES Salient. Weather fine.	
do	7/9/17		Route March by Section; afternoon Barrage Drill, 1 Pack mule Out. to R.E.'s for jobbing trucks covers.	
do	8/9/17		Coy. inspection at 10 a.m. Transport at 11 a.m. by Commanding Officer. Coy. bathed in the evening. Weather dull but fine.	

Army Form C. 2118.

WAR DIARY
or
INTELLIGENCE SUMMARY

(Erase heading not required.)

Vol VI
Sheet 2.

Instructions regarding War Diaries and Intelligence Summaries are contained in F. S. Regs., Part II. and the Staff Manual respectively. Title Pages will be prepared in manuscript.

Place	Date	Hour	Summary of Events and Information	Remarks and references to Appendices
WINNEZEELE	8/9/17		Church parade. 2 O.R. proceeded 3/5 21st Squadron RFC to attend a course of identification of Aircraft. weather fine	
do	10/9/17		Gun Drill on rough ground. O.C. & Adjutant visited Division on grounds chosen by S.O. for this work. Afternoon Barrage Drill weather fine	
do	11/9/17		Morning Tactical Scheme. Nos 3 & 4 Section forming a battery under 2nd Lieut. No 2 Section acted as infantry. D.M.G.O. attended at the scheme. Afternoon cleaning of Gun etc. weather fine & very hot.	
do	12/9/17		Morning Sectional Tactical Exercises including Barrage work. Afternoon — Coy-Drill. Weather — Rain.	
do	13/9/17		Morning. All Ranks Lecture inspected by Lorries Scotchmen paraded whole section. Then Inspection of guns Spare parts & in the afternoon. Firing Drill. Aero Defence from Gun Pit. Missing today Section Ranks together & the enemy.	
do	14/9/17		Still in the afternoon full & again. Scale Cart & Tripods used to Motor Lorry. Refilling Tripods continued and carried G Barre as before in. Company could not obtain them	

Army Form C. 2118.

WAR DIARY
or
INTELLIGENCE SUMMARY
(Erase heading not required.)

Vol VI
Sheet 3

Place	Date	Hour	Summary of Events and Information	Remarks and references to Appendices
WINNEZEELE	14/9/19		Company & Transport Inspection by the C.O. Company Commanders told the morning. Recreation with afternoon. Coy. Ba. Red at the midday. C.O. gave us thank to Padre. Time out drill.	
do.	15/9/19		Church Parade - Time & day off. Relieved by N°2 section at 11 am ou. 2:15	
do.	17/9/19		Morning. Parade over. Lecture. Arrangements. Bany drill. The S.M.V.P. attended.	
do.	18/9/19		Morning. P.T. Tactical exercises under O.C. Afternoon. Cleaning guns, spare parts & equipment. By. Paid.	
do.	19/9/19		Weather fine, cooler. Chermany. P.T., Gun drill, warm up Bon Refer kit in M.S. Kannon, Camps of Stokes guns till 8:30 am. Orders received seven Bany drill. All afternoon. And II. early following morning. We ay rain all night.	
WATOU	20/9/19		Left Camp at WINNEZEELE at 7:30 am. Arrived in new Camp at 12 noon. Marching in STEEN VOORDE, WEE Dt. Enrolic bivouac this Dir. We at WINNES 2:35 E15. le. Reconnaissance. Some rain early in morning.	

COMPG N° 200 M.G. Coy.

WAR DIARY
or
INTELLIGENCE SUMMARY

Army Form C. 2118.

VOL VI
Sheet 4

Place	Date	Hour	Summary of Events and Information	Remarks and references to Appendices
WATOU	21/9/17		Morning. Company paraded & Thanksgiving Service for the successful carrying out of arrangements with Trench Mortars (faulty condemned) returned to S.A.D.O.S and new ones fitted thereon.	
do	22/9/17		Moved into North Area YPRES. Received orders to put 16 guns into the line on night of 23rd/24th. Weather very fine.	
YPRES. N.	23/9/17		OC to reconnoitre new battery position at Shrivon and S. of SOMME. Relief carried out & completed at 9-10 p.m. Coy H.Q's at JASPER FARM. Heavy Shelling about 10th & 12 midnight.	
do	24/9/17		The enemy shelled gun positions with gas projectiles. 17 O.R. slightly gassed. Heavy shelling in the forenoon. Section officers reconnoitred positions & Hill 35 for available Battery positions.	
do	25/9/17		Details at Transport Lines. Goldfish Chateau sent to St. Jean. System of emplacement near of Battery positions to be occupied at night. Telephone communication established between Coy H.Q's at POMMERN CASTLE & R.13 and Coy Battery. Later information received transmitted to officers concerned.	

WAR DIARY or INTELLIGENCE SUMMARY

Army Form C. 2118.

VOL VI Sheet 5.

Place	Date	Hour	Summary of Events and Information	Remarks and references to Appendices
YPRES. N.	26/9/17		All Batteries subjected to very heavy shell fire. Casualties of officers very heavy. Major T. Linfield East. O.C. wounded. 2nd Lt Willis 'B' Battery commander killed. 2nd Lts Withington, Vant, Davies & Storey wounded. 5 O.R. killed. 21 O.R. wounded. Lieut Enode proceeded to Adv. H.Qs at 3 pm to take over the duties of O.C.	
do	27/9/17		Orders from D.M.G.O. to withdraw guns from Battery position & establish headquarters at JASPER FARM & dump all equipment there. H.Q's established at JASPER FARM at 10 am. Here the coy formed Corps Reserve.	
do	28/9/17		Received orders to find a position for 6 guns to take part in an attack by 3rd Div on WINDMILL CABARET. Good positions taken up near DELVA FARM. This order was cancelled about 2.30 pm & Transport Lines were ordered to return to GOLDFISH CHATEAU, arriving there at 10 pm.	
do	29/9/17		Capt Hadcroft rejoined from course at CAMIERS. Commenced reorganisation	

WAR DIARY
or
INTELLIGENCE SUMMARY

Vol VI Sheet 6

Place	Date	Hour	Summary of Events and Information	Remarks and references to Appendices
YPRES N.	29/9/17	Various	Coy made preparations for moving to VLAMERTINGHE No 2 Area	
do	30/9/17		Coy moved to New Area at 9 a.m. Pitched camp by 3 p.m. Hostile Aircraft very active dropping many bombs in the vicinity of Camp. No casualties inflicted in the Area. Received orders to move to STEENBECQUE weather very hot.	

Donald Lieut
for Capt
COMDG. No. 200 M.G. COY

Army Form C. 2118.

WAR DIARY
or
INTELLIGENCE SUMMARY
(Erase heading not required.)

Vol 7

200th Company, Machine Gun Corps.
VOLUME VII.
OCTOBER 1917.

W. Omalie Lieut. & Adjt.
200th Coy. Machine Gun Corps

Army Form C. 2118.

WAR DIARY
or
INTELLIGENCE SUMMARY

(Erase heading not required.)

Instructions regarding War Diaries and Intelligence Summaries are contained in F.S. Regs., Part II. and the Staff Manual respectively. Title Pages will be prepared in manuscript.

VOL VII Sheet 1

Place	Date	Hour	Summary of Events and Information	Remarks and references to Appendices
YPRES N	1/10/17	7 am	Transport move by road to STEENBERQE under Transport Officer arriving at 4pm. Remainder Bttg moves by rail at 9.30 pm to STEENBERQE. Advance party twenty half B and arriving at 2pm by motor lorry. Station severely bombed during entrainment & departure delayed.	Yr. Yr/s/m
STEENBERQE	2/10/17	6 am	Coy de train at STEENBERQE & troops into Billets in village arriving at 7 am. The Divisional Commander at 11.30 am visited the Company and spoke to them regarding the recent operations. Capt J.B. Hastings appointed 2nd in command of the Company in place of Major Seaforth (sent to HQ). Lieut W Emslie being appointed 3rd in command. Auth. A.J. win. no & personnel.	Yr/t
do	3/10/17	10	Company inspected by Commanding Officer. Reorganising casualties checked and re-equipment of men. Total strength of men material found to total 6 officers & 66 O.R. DHQ & returns 2/Lieut Thornton C.O. furnished a report to Divisional Commander on the officers. Recommendations for holowing during recent operations forwarded to Division. Inspection of Transport by C.O. Company detail a/warded out to clean city.	Yr/A
do	4/10/17	11 am	Lieut Wilson, 2/Lieuts Hope, & Nuttall report from M.J. Bass for duty. 3 O.R. reinforcements arrive from M.J. Bass. Orders received warning move to RQMY area.	It
do	5/10/17		Company employed in preparing for move. C.O. sees next officers that than orderlies to Nos 3, 2, 4 Section respectively.	Yr.

2449 Wt. W14957/M90 750,000 1/16 J.B.C. & A. Forms/C.2118/12.

Army Form C. 2118.

WAR DIARY
or
INTELLIGENCE SUMMARY
(Erase heading not required.)

Vol VI Sheet 2

Instructions regarding War Diaries and Intelligence Summaries are contained in F.S. Regs., Part II and the Staff Manual respectively. Title Pages will be prepared in manuscript.

Place	Date	Hour	Summary of Events and Information	Remarks and references to Appendices
SUCRE RESERVE	7/10/19		Company moved to PETIGNY. Transport proceeded with advanceparty by direct route arriving 3pm. Company marched via AIRE 9 metres from there & PETIGNY arriving 8pm. C.S.M. Clegg reports for duty.	9/H
PETIGNY	7/10/19		Church parade - heavy rain 7/Lt C. Bass reports from Base depot re- taken on strength.	9/H
do	8/10/17		Reorganisation re-equipment of company drawn up. Programme for training.	9/H
			Section Officers proceed with Lewis Guns into the line. Necessary arrangement made. Fitted Several Coat Mantlet assembled at Coy H.Q. for the trial of	9/H
do	9/10/19		Cpl Dugan & Pte Nefile. Chap afount Cpl Dugan dismissed. Appologies.	1/BA
do	10/10/19	6 am	C.O. proceeds with C.O. of 177 Inf Bde & new Sector, by car arriving at AVION 12 noon. reports to 3rd Canadian Bde H.Q. re numerous M.G. Coy Commander of Regt Lewis Section	7/B/A
		9 am	Company proceed by route march to temporary billets at MAREST. arriving ad. 1 pm The heavy rain.	
		10pm	C.O. returns.	
MAREST	11/10/17	9am	Company moves from MAREST to temporary billets at MAISNIL CES RUITZ via HOUDAIN arriving 3pm. Slight rain	9/Rift

Army Form C. 2118.

WAR DIARY
or
INTELLIGENCE SUMMARY
(Erase heading not required.)

Vol VII

Instructions regarding War Diaries and Intelligence Summaries are contained in F. S. Regs., Part II. and the Staff Manual respectively. Title Pages will be prepared in manuscript.

Place	Date	Hour	Summary of Events and Information	Remarks and references to Appendices
HAZEBROUCK	17/9/19	9 AM	Company moves by route march from MAROEUIL to CHATEAU DE LA HAIE. Arriving afternoon. In camp for the night. Heavy rain	JH
CHATEAU DE LA HAIE	13/9/19		Company moves to ALBERTA Camp CARENCY. From Chateau arriving about 3 PM. In camp for night. Heavy rain	JH
ALBERTA CAMP	14/9/19		Company moves from ALBERTA Camp to O'DILLON Camp for night. Heavy rain. 4 ORS 415 hours on leave	JH
O'DILLON CAMP	15/9/19		Company moves from O'DILLON Camp to M.G. Camp CARENCY. Relief of Guards revealed by 3rd Canadian M.G. Coy. C.O. proceeds into Ob. go to see M.G. Ramps of HAIE & OEFFERS FARM. Heavy rain	JH
CARENCY	16/9/19		Programme of training drawn up. Waring order received that Coy was to relieve the M.G. Coy in right sector. Return under fifteen officers	JH
do	17/9/19		Coy to proceed to line and interview BC 174 mg Coy regarding relief & fire disposition. Company under sectional training	JH
do	18/9/19		Company inspected by C.O. 2/Lt GIBBS admitted to Hospital and struck off strength 16/11. Thorne evacuated to C.C.S.	JH

2449 Wt. W14957/M90 750,000 1/16 J.B.C. & A. Forms/C.2118/12.

WAR DIARY or INTELLIGENCE SUMMARY

Army Form C. 2118.

Place	Date	Hour	Summary of Events and Information	Remarks and references to Appendices
CARENCY	19/10/17		2/Lt BANDY reports from M.G. Base depot. O.C. in acting & lectures Officer. Afternoon Company taken to elementary musk'ry practice.	19/10/17
do	20/10/17	7am	Orders received regarding relief in foll'n'g day of 17th by the unit. Limber jackets and operation orders issued. Reconn. arrangements made. Orders received to move transport to BOUVIGNY.	20/10/17
		1pm	Coy Transport move to BOUVIGNY.	
		11am	Church parade. 3 hrs.	
do	21/10/17	5.30pm	Coy moves off for relief arriving at LIEVIN 6.30pm. Relief reported complete at 10.7pm. Disposition of Company as follows:— "D" Section on left under 2/Lt HOLE. "B" Section in Centre under 2/Lt NUTTALL. "C" Section on Right under 2/Lt BRUCE. Stacks:- POLAR - PAGAN - PARIS - POODLE & many taking over the guns ABBOLOM - MILL HILL - FOREST HILL - GEORGE ROBEY. ADJUTANT - ALIDAM Rest taking over the guns:- BICLY - SOUCHEZ - RESERVOIR. A Section are attached to & MOULIN. Two gun teams of "A" Section under 2/Lt BANDY as Inspection officer, Coy Headquarters under 2/Lt GIVENS with 2/Lt BANDY acts as 2.i.c. Company. Shots taken over at M 23.d.59. Lieut WILSON	21/10/17
LENS	22/10/17	9am	O.C. visits RESERVOIR gun and Right group.	
		10am	O.C. visits Bde. H.Q. + Battalion H.Q.	
		5pm	O.C. visits CENTRE Group - Situation normal. Weather Wind W.S.W. Stormy + rain	

WAR DIARY
or
INTELLIGENCE SUMMARY

(Erase heading not required.)

Army Form C. 2118.

Place	Date	Hour	Summary of Events and Information	Remarks and references to Appendices
LENS	27/10/19	8am	O.C. visits Left Front of Guns. Sees Bde H.Q. regarding change of gun position of Maroon gun & right front gun. G.O.C. Cattis in afternoon. Work continued on improved C.T. to Left Group H.Q. looking party sent.	JH
		5pm	O.C. visits HILL HILL & HOOVER Gun - reconnoitre position for a possible new gun at MOULIN. Harassing fire during night by 9 guns on LENS ROAD rehappened - 12,000 rounds expended during the night. Situation such anych - weather stormy rain.	
do	23/10/19	8am	O.C. visits right front & decides on adding a changing - Enemy artillery very active during day. Work commenced on FOREST HILL gun. Also new shelter for gun team connected to soocres gun.	JH
		3pm	O.C. visits Centre guns. Will fix Lewis shields - Six guns engaged in harassing enemy approaches during night 1800 rounds expended - Situation normal - Weather clearing with cold unsettled showers. Wind W.N.W.	
do	24/10/19	7am	O.C. visits Mouser Gun & reconnoitre right extreme sector for new position. Also visits Left sector Lewis M.G. firing during night very active. C.T. to POLAR deepened - FORESTHILL emplacement continues work on dugout. Situation normal. Hostile artillery less active.	JH
do	25/10/19	9am	O.C. visits front and right sector. Harassing fire continues, situation normal - Raining.	JH

WAR DIARY
or
INTELLIGENCE SUMMARY

Army Form C. 2118.

Place	Date	Hour	Summary of Events and Information	Remarks and references to Appendices
LEENS Suffering	26/10/17	7 am	O.C. tracks from position – Refraction slightly across. Alignment from tracks to theor. alignment made there adjust. N 25 B 16 (map sheet map 36 C SW). H.Q. in afternoon. G.O.C. visits Company & attends training situation around! POLAR – POODLE – ASSOCIAM – MILLHILL in training. Situation around. Rifle & Rocket fires used in harassing fire – 18,100 rds expended Hostile aircraft active. R/G fun burst over engaged in A.A. work. 3000 rds fired + 1 F & A flares to assist A/C to locate hostile Aircraft. Return normal.	9H
do	27/10/17	8 am	OC to Reg Group. Am. ampo visits R/C to visit left M.G. Coy em co-operation. Work continuing on emplacements & dugouts – fourteen being made. Harassing fire as opportunity. L 6 M G & Lewis Guns used. Situation normal. Weather rainy during night. Enemy Artillery during the day – Wind S.W.	9H
do	28/10/17	8 am	OC to Centre Group in morning – & Ref went in morning. FORREST HOUSE Engineer Completed during night – less activity during night compared to harrows by this enemy to work on emplacements. Situation normal. Weather fine. O.C. to Left Group. Night firing position of POODLE from N.S. by S.G. to Beauer adjacent from N 25 B 25 – C.O. to C.H.Q. O.C. to work on keg target – Regt slight	9B†
do	29/10/17	7 am	Right firing position moved to 150 yds left. C.O.O. visits C.H.Q. to Right Group at night. Adjust from name to N25 B25 – Situation unchanged. Enemy artillery Rew irrigant to forcey. Completed Enemy activity.	9H†

WAR DIARY
or
INTELLIGENCE SUMMARY

Army Form C. 2118.

Place	Date	Hour	Summary of Events and Information	Remarks and references to Appendices
LENS	30/10/17	3 am	Lt. Col. Ryder Grant O.C. 6 Brigade – interview with F.O.O. regarding M.G. Batteries OP.F.O.'s, Sub Company and methods complete. Form of section Lith. Co. Returns. A.Q. 11 p.m. Harassing fire with 4 guns on enemy approach Lens – in bridge at Laurel – 10,000 rounds were fired during the night toward Lens in front rear ASHANTI CAR UNES FARM.	
do	31/10/17	10 am	Operation order received regarding the discharge of gas by 11th Div. on the left & 39 Division – necessary cautionary orders issued – Orders issued to Sections for shot during night event to prevent German relief. Orders issued with artillery & harassing fire throughout the night 25000 & Section officers & calculation issued – Harassing fire Extended 11.30 p.m. 7 guns concentrated on 20 B 79 (report LENS 36 c SW1). Weather fine, wind still. Situation normal & unchanged.	

J.B. Harvey Capt.
Comdg 200 M.G. Coy.

ORIGINAL

Army Form C. 2118.

WAR DIARY
of
INTELLIGENCE SUMMARY
(Erase heading not required.)

5 9 Dv

Vol 8

VOLUME VIII.
NOVEMBER, 1917.

200TH COMPANY, MACHINE GUN CORPS.

W. Fowler
Lieut. & Adj t.
200th Coy.
Machine Gun Corps.

Place	Date	Hour	Summary of Events and Information	Remarks and references to Appendices

Instructions regarding War Diaries and Intelligence Summaries are contained in F. S. Regs., Part II. and the Staff Manual respectively. Title Pages will be prepared in manuscript.

Army Form C. 2118.

WAR DIARY
or
INTELLIGENCE SUMMARY
(Erase heading not required.)

VOL VIII
Sheet 1.

Instructions regarding War Diaries and Intelligence Summaries are contained in F. S. Regs., Part II. and the Staff Manual respectively. Title Pages will be prepared in manuscript.

Place	Date	Hour	Summary of Events and Information	Remarks and references to Appendices
LENS	1/11/17	10/AM	OC visits Batt. HQ. and Right-front gun — Boy very quiet. A few geo shells fell near RESERVOIR gun — No casualties. Sketch received from Brigade of our proposed S.O.S. lines. Shoemakers report punctures. Casualties nil. Weather Normal — Intellin — fair - Wind - N. gentle MILD	WE.
LENS	2/11/17	5 AM	DINGO together with OC visited gun positions in LEFT & CENTRE groups. Day quiet. Enemy MGs active during the night. Artillery activity quiet. No casualties. Situation normal - Weather fair. Wind - N. gentle MILD	WE.
LENS	3/11/17		MILL HILL - ABSALOM - RESERVOIR gun positions shelled - no casualties. Good rounds	WE.
		12 noon	harassing fire fired during night. First Army Standing Orders issued to section commanders. LT ENSLIE arrives to act as EO rebtbs ThCO proceeds to CHARENCY before proceeding on	
		2 PM	leave. CO + 2 i/c command visited guns in LEFT group.	
		8-9 PM	Several gas shells dropped about M 30 d 19. No casualties. Situation Normal - Weather dull rainy - WIND - NIL	
LENS	4/11/17	5 AM	Acting CO visited gun positions in CENTRE & RIGHT groups. 2/Lt BANDEY reconnoitred position for new gun on Rly embankment near A in ALOOF TRENCH. Report sent in to BHQ. 10,000 rounds harassing fire fired during night. No casualties. Situation Normal - Weather fair - WIND - MILD.	WE.

WAR DIARY
or
INTELLIGENCE SUMMARY

Army Form C. 2118.

Vol VII Sheet 2.

Place	Date	Hour	Summary of Events and Information	Remarks and references to Appendices
LENS	5/11/17	noon	Having drawn SOS lines from DMGO, all calculations worked out. Checked guns laid by 6pm. Harassing fire been rounds fired during night. Signal small gas bombardment by enemy artillery during the night. Balloon carrying parachute nearby. Station which seemed to fall near LEFT SEC HQ. Weather good. Wind West. E Casualties nil - situation normal.	W.E.
		4pm to 12mt	Empty cases collected. Preparations made for Relief. The NCO's of gun teams arrive from 147th Coy.	
LENS	6/11/17	5AM	Relg OC visits MOULIN gun centre group.	
		6PM	OC 147th Coy arrives at CoyHQ. Sections follow & RELIEF is carried out by sections all TRIPODS, BELT BOXES & water cans together with trench stores, checked & handed over. Sections move off independently on relief. RELIEF reported complete at 10pm. Last retail arrives at CARENCY.	N.E.
CARENCY	7/11/17	9AM	Coy inspected. Guns cleaned & braziers taken. O.C. goes with DMGO & 2/Lt Mott Mulhal Bartry to LENS sector to reconnoitre new positions returning 4pm. Weather Rainy & Dull.	N.E.
"	8/11/17	9AM	Coy training. Gun drill brothers by SO's. QED goes to BHQ to confer with DMGO on Defence Scheme. Weather - Wet	N.E.

WAR DIARY
or
INTELLIGENCE SUMMARY

Volume VIII SHEET III

(Erase heading not required.)

Army Form C. 2118.

Place	Date	Hour	Summary of Events and Information	Remarks and references to Appendices
CARENCY	10/11/19	9AM	O/C O + 2/LT BANDEY to Bttl. Defence Scheme. Company training under S.O.S. (under)	NW
		4PM	Pilots roamed of S.A.A. taken to Advanced Coy HQ at LIEVIN under 2/LT NUTTALL. Weather - mist in morning, fine later.	
do	11/11/19	9AM	Preparations made for firing on range at MARQUEFFLES FARM. 2/4 MOLE marches Coy to LIEVIN & proceeds to SAA in reserve gun positions. Report sent to DMGO when complete. Weather Dull but fine.	WE
do	12/11/19	7AM	Coy Parade for field firing on Range. A+B sections firing. C+D sections in butts. Firing takes place under DMGO's instruction & supervision. Coy arrives back at CARENCY at 8pm. Weather Fine West wind. MILD.	NW
do	13/11/19	9AM	Gun cleaning & belt filling. Sections try S.R.s. Scheme of Sector Handover Bombing.	W
		2PM	Bathing parade by sections at Divisional Baths. Weather Rainy Dull.	
do	14/11/19	7AM	Coy parade for field firing on Range. B+D sections firing. A+C sections in butts. Firing takes place under DMGO's instruction & supervision. Coy arrives back at CARENCY at 8pm. Preliminary orders received for Coy to be prepared to move SOUTH. Weather fine Cold. Wind Frost.	NW

WAR DIARY or INTELLIGENCE SUMMARY

Army Form C. 2118.

VOLUMN VIII
Sheet 4

Place	Date	Hour	Summary of Events and Information	Remarks and references to Appendices
EN RENCY	15/4/17	9AM	Gun cleaning + rifle firing. Lectures by S.O.s. Issue of Sun parts, 1 Sectioris.	105°
do	16/4/17	9AM	800000 rounds of S.A.A. drawn from Dump. Weather fine. Mild. Preparations made for movement. Orders received to move to HERMAVILLE. Lt Wilson sent as billeting officer in advance. Weather fine.	105°
do	17/4/17	9AM / 12noon	Preparations made for moving. Coy Parade marched to HERMAVILLE. River SCARPE not crossed before 2pm. Transport billeted at HERMAVILLE, remainder of Coy at TILLOY-LES-HERMAVILLE. Movement under orders of 174th Brigade. Arrival reported to Brigade at 8PM.	106°
TILLOY-LES-HERMAVILLE	18/4/17	9AM / 12noon	Coy in billets at TILLOY. Lt WILSON sent in advance to BLAIREVILLE under orders of 176th Brigade for movement of Coy the following day.	107°
	19/4/17	9AM / 4:30PM / 9:30PM	Preparations for move. Coy paraded for movement to BLAIREVILLE under orders of 176th Brigade. MAIN ROAD at BEAUMETZ not to be crossed before 6PM. Coy arrive at No 2 Camp BLAIREVILLE	108°

WAR DIARY
or
INTELLIGENCE SUMMARY

Army Form C. 2118.

VOLUMN VIII SHEET 5.

Place	Date	Hour	Summary of Events and Information	Remarks and references to Appendices
BLAIREVILLE	25/11/17	9 AM	Orders received to prepare for movement at short notice & entrain by strength return to be sent to 178th Brigade. Surplus stores Trench Mortars dumped in fort in (X.26.b.48)	WD
		10 AM	Coy to discharge 1st Lt WHITTAL NOBLE sent out to reconnoitre road to COURCELLES-LE-COMTE. LIBRYCE sent to DADOS to draw pack saddles & leather gaitors which were not received.	
Do	26/11/17	9 AM	Coy standing by for orders of movement.	WD
		4 PM	Orders for movement received. Coy move off at 1.30 p.m. to COURCELLES-LE-COMTE arriving at 11 p.m. Billeted in tents 1 mile from Mayor Office. Rather fine.	
COURCELLES LE COMTE	27/11/17	10 AM	The C.O. reports back from leave. Coy standing by awaiting orders to move. Rather dull with slight rain.	WD
	27/11/17	9 AM	Orders received for movement to ETRICOURT AREA.	
		2 PM	Transport leaves under command of T.O. 1st moon to EQUANCOURT	6 WD
		2.30 pm	Coy Parade March to BIHUCOURT-W & then entrain with 178th Inf Brigade & proceed to FINS arriving 5 p.m. & are directed to billets in DESSART WOOD. This was found to be occupied by the 174th I Brigade Coy proceed to EQUANCOURT where they are billeted in huts under 178th Brigade. (Camp B.12.)	
EQUANCOURT	28/11/17		Kit Inspection by S.Os. Gun cleaning & checking of equipments. Barrack Drill in afternoon. Weather cold & showery.	WD

Army Form C. 2118.

WAR DIARY
or
INTELLIGENCE SUMMARY
(Erase heading not required.)

VOL VIII.
Sheet 6.

Instructions regarding War Diaries and Intelligence Summaries are contained in F.S. Regs., Part II. and the Staff Manual respectively. Title Pages will be prepared in manuscript.

Place	Date	Hour	Summary of Events and Information	Remarks and references to Appendices
EQUANCOURT	25/11/17	9am	Church parade in Church Army hut. in the morning. Aft. noon inspection Brigadier General Stanfield D.C.O.C. INFIBDE. WEATHER Cold + wet.	WR
do	26/11/17	"	Tactical Exercise in the morning. C.O. to reconnoitre line near BOURLON WOOD. Adjutant to D.A.D.O.S. at NURLU. to intendt in the afternoon. 4 Section officers to 9th Armoured Formation for Tactical Exercises without troops. Weather very wet.	WR
do	27/11/17		Action on Park Saddles for the Offensive. Range Today under R.T. N.C.O. for instruction testing of instruments. S/s Givens to Cpn Rail Station. Weather Still showery runny cold.	WR
do	28/11/17 am		Received instruction to send 2 guns to DUMP at K 20 a 2.2. for forwarding. 4 DUMP of ENEMY AIRCRAFT. Guns in position at 7.30 am. Received orders to move to HAVRINCOURT WOOD.	WR
do	29/11/19 am		Orders received to proceed to HAVRINCOURT WOOD at 1-30 pm. Co. marched to sent tables, which was received at 12.30 pm. Mof R/f. D.9.d. arrival, no accommodation provided. I billed at P.16.6.9. arriving about 10-30 pm Weather fine. WEATHER FINE	WR

Army Form C. 2118.

WAR DIARY
or
INTELLIGENCE SUMMARY
(Erase heading not required.)

Vol VIII Sht-7.

Place	Date	Hour	Summary of Events and Information	Remarks and references to Appendices
HAVRINCOURT WOOD.	30/10/17	9am	Gun Cleaning etc, awaiting orders for move into line. Hostile artillery shelled HAVRINCOURT WOOD intermittently during the day. Several landing near Transport Lines, moved Transport Lines nearer wood at 2 pm.	WE

Army Form C. 2118.

ORIGINAL
WAR DIARY
or
INTELLIGENCE SUMMARY.
(Erase heading not required.)

VOLUME IX
DECEMBER, 1917
200TH COY. MACHINE GUN CORPS.

J. Showing, Capt.
COMDG. No. 200 M.G. Coy.

Army Form C. 2118.

WAR DIARY
or
INTELLIGENCE SUMMARY

VOL IX Sheet I.

(Erase heading not required.)

Place	Date	Hour	Summary of Events and Information	Remarks and references to Appendices
HAVRINCOURT WOOD.	1/12/17	4 am	Orders were received at 7 p.m. 30/11/17 to send 8 guns into the line at FLESQUIERES at any time left within a ½ hour notice. Lieut. Wilson. The remaining half Coy then proceeded to Q.Q.A.4.I. and bivouaced in the open, no other accommodation being available. O.C. to Advanced D.H.Q's. Coy. H.Q's + ½ Coy took over lines vacated by 61st M.G. Coy. 4. O.R's wounded. WEATHER – DRY	1/5/6
"	2/12/17	9 am	Coy under orders to move at short notice. Limber parking in the morning + dumping of any surplus gun gear. D.M.G.O. to see O.C. in the morning. Arrangements completed in the event of a move. O.C. + 1 Section Officer proceeds to LA JUSTICE re relief with 174th M.G.C. 1 O.R. killed. Weather stormy, rainy.	1/5
"	3/12/17	9 am	Relief of 6 guns in the line by 175th M.G. Coy. D.M.G.O. wires. O.C. that O.C. 175 M.G. Coy killed to-night + sends one officer to report to 178 Inf. Bde. H.Q's to arrange relief. 2nd Command to FLESQUIERES. WEATHER. Uncool.	1/5
LA JUSTICE	4/12/17	4 am	Coy relieved 174th M.G. Coy. in the line at BOURLON WOOD with 16 guns. Completes in the morning. 18 The evening shelled BOURLON WOOD heavily with gas shells. One mule killed + one wounded at Coy. H.Q's LA JUSTICE. Considerable movement seen in FONTAINE. WEATHER. Fine but cold.	1/2

Army Form C. 2118.

WAR DIARY
or
INTELLIGENCE SUMMARY

Vol IX
Sheet 2.

(Erase heading not required.)

Instructions regarding War Diaries and Intelligence Summaries are contained in F. S. Regs., Part II. and the Staff Manual respectively. Title Pages will be prepared in manuscript.

Place	Date	Hour	Summary of Events and Information	Remarks and references to Appendices
LA JUSTICE	4/12/17	10 am	Orders received to withdraw from forward positions BOURLON WOOD. Company returned to Coy H.Qs in HAVRINCOURT WOOD. C.O. Y/Col Bardsley received at H.Qs 173rd M.G. Coy of FLESQUIERES. WEATHER FINE. Sent Capt. 2nd Lieut S.G. Smith & B/Lt J. Ellis reported in from Base Depot	W.E.
HAVRINCOURT WOOD	5/12/17	4 am	Orders received at 3am to take up 16 gun position in front and at FLESQUIERES. All arrangements made for Company proceeding to the line at 5pm. Guns in position at 11-30 p.m. 8 Vickers-Canneliers. B/W Coy. H.Qs in Sunken Road between RIBECOURT & FLESQUIERES. Rem. Coy H.Q. in HAVRINCOURT WOOD. WEATHER FINE. Hostile artillery was active throughout the day so heavily on FLESQUIERES & town. A protest by an aircraft that the enemy was massing Opp-	W.E.
FLESQUIERES	6/12/17		3 pm the enemy attempted an attack in FLESQUIERES but were at once opp- with M.G. triple fire. The M.G.'s fired 40,000 rounds inflicting enormous casualties on the enemy, a prisoner captured during the attack states that practically all his battalion were casualties. No further attack was made. WEATHER: FINE. We had very cas. 2. O.R.S. Wounded. S/Lt R. Weymler Gr.	W.E.
FLESQUIERES	7/12/17	4 am	A considerable amount of enemy movement was seen in the	

WAR DIARY
or
INTELLIGENCE SUMMARY
(Erase heading not required.)

Vol IX
Sect-3

Army Form C. 2118.

Place	Date	Hour	Summary of Events and Information	Remarks and references to Appendices
FLESQUIERES	7/11/17		neighbourhood of LA JUSTICE firing Verey lights sniping targets. M.G.s were laid on spots where enemy were seen to pass, no[?] casualties were inflicted on the enemy. WEATHER - showery, dull.	
FLESQUIERES	8/11/17	11am	The enemy was less active than usual [?] in the front. HAVRINCOURT WOOD & METZ was shelled intermittently during the day by 4.7 H.V. Shells 5·9 & 4·2s traffic being held up at intervals. WEATHER. Showery.	
FLESQUIERES	9/11/17	4am	Enemy Aircraft were very active flying very low & busy with MGs on our trenches & signalling with white lights, presumably to Hostile artillery opens fire on our positions. 2 enemy aeroplanes were brought down by M.G. fire. WEATHER FINE.	
FLESQUIERES	10/11/17	4 am	Enemy very quiet & nothing to report. Orders received that 174TH MG Coy were to relieve us on the night 10/11. Transport leave Coy HQrs lost night & Recon Coy HQrs of 174TH MG Coy at LECHELLE at 3 pm. A[?] [?] Company moving not of the Church	

Army Form C. 2118.

WAR DIARY
or
INTELLIGENCE SUMMARY
(Erase heading not required.)

Vol IX
Sect-4

Place	Date	Hour	Summary of Events and Information	Remarks and references to Appendices
FLESQUIERES	10/1/17		Relief completed 8-30 p.m. Company arrived at LECHELLE at 11-45 p.m. Hot soup served out to men. Weather: fine.	WS
LECHELLE	11/1/17	9 a.m.	Gun cleaning + general cleaning of equipment etc. A-Aircraft gun mounted in camp. Enemy aircraft seen over YPRES about 6 a.m. + antiques seen at bursts no casualties were inflicted. Weather FINE	WS
LECHELLE	12/1/17	9 a.m.	Inspection of Guns, Spare parts + Signalling gear by Commanding Officer in the morning reconnaissance in the afternoon. D.M.G.O. visited DUMPS at O.C. coy re Anti-aircraft gun to be taken near YPRES + BUS. Weather: fine	WS
LECHELLE	13/1/17	9 a.m.	Guns of "B" Section to Anti-Aircraft position 2 at YPRES 2 at BUS. Gun in position at 10 a.m. Gun Drill in the morning. Recreation in the afternoon. Lieut F.C. Wilson + 221 Nuttall proceeded on leave to U.K. Weather: fine	WS

2449 Wt. W14957/Mgo 750,000 1/16 J.B.C. & A. Forms/C.2118/12

WAR DIARY
or
INTELLIGENCE SUMMARY
(Erase heading not required.)

Army Form C. 2118.

Place	Date	Hour	Summary of Events and Information	Remarks and references to Appendices
LECHELLE	14/7/19	9 am	Elementary Gun work & Company Drill with morning Parades in the afternoon. 200 parcels from Queen Alexandra's Field Force Fund received & issued out to all N.C.O.s — C.O. to Division HQ. Warning order received respecting relief on night 16/17th of 17th by 174 MG Coy in the line. Weather fine	6E
LECHELLE	15/7/19	9 am	Gun Cleaning & making preparations for proceeding to the line next day. D.M.G.O. visits O.C. re relief etc. Weather fine	6E
LECHELLE	16/7/19	9 am	Coy proceeded to the line at 2pm leaving 2in Command & Transport at LECHELLE. 18th M.G.Coy took over HQrs at LECHELLE. On 2pm Transport proceeded to LONE FARM near NEUVILLE forming Report Pt. Adv Coy HQrs in Sunken Road between FLESQUIERES & RIBECOURT. Relief completed at 10-30 pm in casualties. Weather fine	A18
FLESQUIERES	17/7/19	4 am	The Enemy had guidance down considerably since last report in line indirect. Targets were chosen & 30,000 rounds fired during barrages which fog prevented observing the day which was taken full advantage.	

WAR DIARY
or
INTELLIGENCE SUMMARY
(Erase heading not required.)

Army Form C. 2118.

Vol IX Sheet 6

Place	Date	Hour	Summary of Events and Information	Remarks and references to Appendices
FLESQUIERES	17/9/17	am	of by bn. S in suspected dumps. RIBECOURT was shelling with 5.9" about 6 pm. Weather fine but very foggy. O.C. omits Regt Tps.	WD
FLESQUIERES	18/9/17	4 am	Brigadier General Commanding 177 Inf Bde accompanied O.C. round various Coys at 6 am. The Commanding in Cape Cap H.Q.s, however, unusually quiet during morning, afternoon & all. From bk. Shelled Sunken road near Coy H.Q.s with 4.2's, 5.9's & 8" ordnance. Only one direct hit was attained on the road evidently the Sunken Road was the target. Weather fine, fairly clear slightly foggy. 15,600 rounds field artillery ammunition known to have been expended in the night today.	WD 658
FLESQUIERES	19/9/17		Reports from our Aeroplanes received this Brigade that considerable amount of new road has been made near ORIVAL WOOD. Same were details [?] of fire in various parts of wood. 20,000 rounds being total fired. Enemy commenced searching for our Battn. with light hows & 77's during am. with little damage done. Weather fine. Casualties nil.	658

Army Form C. 2118.

WAR DIARY
or
INTELLIGENCE SUMMARY

(Erase heading not required.)

Vol. IX
Sheet - 7

Instructions regarding War Diaries and Intelligence Summaries are contained in F. S. Regs., Part II. and the Staff Manual respectively. Title Pages will be prepared in manuscript.

Place	Date	Hour	Summary of Events and Information	Remarks and references to Appendices
FLESQUIERES	20/11/17	4am	Back areas were shelled throughout the morning. TRESCAULT - METZ road being the objective. FLESQUIERES was shelled frequently with 5.9's. The usual harassing fire on selected targets was carried out during the night. 17,500 rounds being fired. 1 O.R. killed & enemy sniper. Weather fine & good observation enabled several of our enemy movement.	W.G.
FLESQUIERES	21/11/17	4am	Both British & enemy aircraft active. Hostile planes flying very low & firing many air fights taking place. One enemy aeroplane brought down in flames. Enemy very quiet throughout the day. Weather front. O.C. various gp. Comp. 13,500 rounds gun mounts leading to Bertincourt factory.	W.G.
FLESQUIERES	22/11/17	4am	Considerable movement was seen near Ribécourt factory, but little activity beyond this to the extreme front. Battle critique was given before then moved Rec. Coy. HQs moved back to BERTINCOURT & four reduced. by 141st M.G.Coy. Gun teams arriving at BERTINCOURT at 11-45pm. Orders received for the relief of remaining guns tomorrow in the 24/2/17. by 52 M.G.Coy. Weather fine, very frosty.	W.G.
FLESQUIERES	23/11/17	8am	Trengaport & Quarters proceeded to ROQUIGNY at 9am. Gun Teams	W.G.

WAR DIARY
or
INTELLIGENCE SUMMARY

Army Form C. 2118.

Vol IX
Sheet 8

Place	Date	Hour	Summary of Events and Information	Remarks and references to Appendices
FLESQUIERES	23/12/17	4 a.m.	remained at BERTINCOURT for remainder of Company serving out of the line. Enemy shelled FLESQUIERES during raid. Signaller Cpl. being wounded whilst repairing wires. 52 M.G. Coy arrived at Coy HQ at 6 p.m. relief completed at 8.30 p.m. Coy arrived at BERTINCOURT at 11 p.m. Enemy aircraft dropped 3 bombs in BERTINCOURT at 8 p.m. killing one wounding 6. of another unit. Weather fine but still frosty.	W.B.
BERTINCOURT	24/12/17	9 a.m.	Transport proceeded at 9 a.m. to ACHIET LE GRAND on way to Rest Area staying there for the night. The Coy marched from BERTINCOURT to ROCQUIGNY arriving 1 p.m. Orders received to entrain at BAPAUME at 11 a.m. on 25/12/17 en route for TINCQUES. Weather thawing.	W.B.
ROCQUIGNY	25/12/17	7 a.m.	Company paraded in full marching order at 7 a.m. and marched to BAPAUME arriving 10-30 a.m., entrained at 11-30 a.m. arriving TINCQUES at 4 p.m. detrained marched to MAIZIERES arriving 6-30 p.m. Our final destination. Billets very good. Weather favouring very hard.	W.B.

Army Form C. 2118.

WAR DIARY
or
INTELLIGENCE SUMMARY

Vol IX Sheet 9

(Erase heading not required.)

Instructions regarding War Diaries and Intelligence Summaries are contained in F. S. Regs., Part II. and the Staff Manual respectively. Title Pages will be prepared in manuscript.

Place	Date	Hour	Summary of Events and Information	Remarks and references to Appendices
MAIZIÈRES	26/12/17	9 am	Holiday for all units in Div.	WD
MAIZIÈRES	27/12/17	9 am	Gun cleaning. General clean up of gun for experimental clip, harness. Remainder in afternoon. Company turn turned out for on Weather - fine	WD
MAIZIÈRES	28/12/17	9 am	Elementary gun work. M.C. Drill. Squad Drill & T. Lecture by S.Os in the morning. Recreation in the afternoon. Weather fine	WD
MAIZIÈRES	29/12/17	9 am	Company inspection by Commanding Officer. Equipment, Drill. Recreation in the afternoon. Weather fine	WD
MAIZIÈRES	30/12/17	9 am	Church parade. Recreation in the afternoon. Weather: fine	WD
MAIZIÈRES	31/12/17	9 am	Gunners Gun drill. Elementary drill. Junior NCOs under CSM. Lecture by S.Os on discipline. Recreation in the afternoon. Weather: fine	WD

2449 Wt. W14957/M90 750,000 1/16 J.B.C. & A. Forms/C.2118/12.

Army Form C. 2118.

ORIGINAL WAR DIARY
or
INTELLIGENCE SUMMARY.
(Erase heading not required.)

Vol 10

VOLUME X

JANUARY, 1918.

200TH COMPANY, MACHINE GUN CORPS.

B Hastings Capt
COMDG. No. 200 M.G. COY.

ORDERLY ROOM
Date 1/2/18
No. 200 MACHINE GUN COMPANY

Instructions regarding War Diaries and Intelligence Summaries are contained in F. S. Regs., Part II. and the Staff Manual respectively. Title pages will be prepared in manuscript.

Place	Date	Hour	Summary of Events and Information	Remarks and references to Appendices

Army Form C. 2118.

WAR DIARY
or
INTELLIGENCE SUMMARY

Vol X.
Sheet 1.

(Erase heading not required.)

Instructions regarding War Diaries and Intelligence Summaries are contained in F. S. Regs., Part II. and the Staff Manual respectively. Title Pages will be prepared in manuscript.

Place	Date	Hour	Summary of Events and Information	Remarks and references to Appendices
MAIZIERES	1/1/18	9 am	Judging distance & recognition of Targets. Lecture by S.O.'s on Fire direction. Squad & Arm drill in the morning. Recreation of officers in the afternoon. Reconds of officers taken at MAIZIERES (from PETIT HOUVIN). Weather: fine.	W.R.
MAIZIERES	2/1/18	9 am	Inspection of guns by Commanding Officer, elementary Gunwork under N.C.O.s. Lecture by Commanding Officer for all officers. Tactical Scheme without guns the morning. Recreation in the afternoon. Completion under R.T. N.C.O. Weather: fine.	W.R.
MAIZIERES	3/1/18	9 am	Fitting of equipments. Inspection of Transport by Commanding Officer. Tactical Scheme with guns under S.O.s. & Lecture in the morning. Lecture by Commanding Officer to all S.O.s. Subject Map Reading. Route march in the afternoon.	W.R.
MAIZIERES	4/1/18	9 am	Coy Comders. & men. Weather fine. 1 Section to M.G. Range (elementary practice). Elementary Gun work. Tactical Scheme in the morning. Football competition in the afternoon. Lt. Col. Mole proceeded on leave to U.K. Clothing issued to B. C. & D Subs. Weather: fine	W.R.

Army Form C. 2118.

WAR DIARY
or
INTELLIGENCE SUMMARY
(Erase heading not required.)

Vol X Sheet 2.

Place	Date	Hour	Summary of Events and Information	Remarks and references to Appendices
MAIZIERES	5/1/18	9am	Preparatory Orders for move by Tactical Trains received. 1 Section & M.G. Range (Elementary practices) Cleaning of S.A.A. packing Kitchen. Roads. With Transport March'n Extern from Linhen. Recreation in the afternoon. Weather: fine.	W²
do	6/1/18	9am	Church Parades in the morning. Inspection by Commanding Officer in the afternoon. Company Pay at 7pm. Weather: fine.	W²
do	7/1/18	9am	One Section to M.G. Range. Coulois Drill & Barrage Drill. Lecture to N.C.O's by Commanding Officer. Elementary Gun work under Section Sgts. Squad T. Arms Drill. Junior N.C.O's under C.S.M. in the morning. Physical training in the afternoon. Weather: fine in the morning. Rain in the evening.	W²
do	8/1/18	9am	Route March - Action from Limber. Inspection of Rifts. L.A.A.R by Armourer Sgt Physical training in the afternoon. Weather: very rainy	W²
do	9/1/18	9am	One Section to M.G. Range. Ironwork Action & Mechanism. Gun Drill with Box Respirators on. Packing of Limbers. Football Competition in the afternoon. Weather: Pouring in the morning.	W²

2449 Wt. W14957/M90 750,000 1/16 J.B.C. & A. Forms/C.2118/12.

WAR DIARY
or
INTELLIGENCE SUMMARY.
(Erase heading not required.)

Army Form C. 2118.

Vol I. Sheet - 3

Place	Date	Hour	Summary of Events and Information	Remarks and references to Appendices
MAZIERES	10/1/18	9am	1 Section to M.G. Range (Edmondmy machine) Advanced Gun work under Selected arrangements in the morning. Physical Training in the afternoon. Weather: Snow frost	W.E.
do	11/1/18	9am	Barrage Drill. Laying & Gunnery Chronometer. Inspection of Guns & transport by Commanding Officer. Lecture by Section Officers & Lectures subject: Fire Direction. Junior NCOs in the Company Sergt Major in the morning. Remainder in the afternoon Instruction & Attack received Light Mgs (reading in reciprocating Course) at HUMBER CAMPS on the 15TH Weather Snow frost (Army Orders)	W.E.
do	12/1/18	9am	Barrage Drill. Lecture by S.O. Subject Fire Direction Signal & Arms Drill in the morning. Rode march with Section Transport Autumn in the afternoon Weather: Camp sites wet	W.E.
do	13/1/18	9am	Church Parade in the morning. Inspection of Company by Canady Officer in the afternoon. Weather: Raining slightly	W.E.
do	14/1/18	9am	Lewis Recognition of Targets. Barrage Drill. Squad & Gun Drill in the morning. Football Competition in the afternoon Weather. Wet.	W.E.
do	15/1/18	9am	Company Tactical Schemes. Lewis and return Carriers Weather Subjects	W.E.

WAR DIARY

Vol X Sheet 4

Place	Date	Hour	Summary of Events and Information	Remarks and references to Appendices
MAZIÈRES	15/1/18	9am	2/Lt Ellis, 1 NCO & two lorries proceeded to ESTREE WAMIN & there lorry picked them up & conveyed them to HUMBER CAMPS. Company pay 2-4pm	WE
Do	16/1/18	9am	Inspection of Company webbing. Transport by Company Officer. Platoons & Squad Games part & afternoon, the morning, to select football competition by the Companies & pick up players for teams not in for the Divisional Challenge Cup. Weather – Showery	WE
Do	17/1/18	9am	Machine gunners, Lewis Gun, Gas Drill, Barrage Drill & Squad training all in the new unit. Company football team practise played in 2 Rounds Divisional Challenge Cup at 2.30pm. Result – the woods 1 goal – Coy 1-6 Corners. Protest lodged by the woods match the replayed. Weather – fine trails	WE
Do	18/1/18	9am	Layrie of Lewis by Corporal. Lecture by C.O. to all officers. Elementary Gun Work made. Lecture by Sgt. Lecture by S.O.'s Subject M. Gun on Defence in the morning. Football in the afternoon. Weather – Showery.	WE
Do	19/1/18	9am	Coy Tactical Scheme from 8:30am to 1:30pm. 5 Reinforcements reported from Base. Football Match with the woods replayed. Result – Showwoods 1- Coy 0. Weather – Fine	WE

WAR DIARY or INTELLIGENCE SUMMARY

Army Form C. 2118.

Vol X
Sheet 5

Place	Date	Hour	Summary of Events and Information	Remarks and references to Appendices
MAZIERES	20/1/18	9 am	Church parade in the morning. Inspection of Company with Transport by Commanding Officer in the afternoon. Football after inspection. 6 men proceeded on leave to U.K. Weather fine & mild.	68
do	21/1/18	9 am	Baths for Coy from 9 & 11 am at MAZIERES. Squad arms drill in the morning. Football in the afternoon. Weather very showery.	68
do	22/1/18	9 am	Cleaning of Guns, Limbers & equipments. Inspection by G.O.C. 59TH DIVISION. The General expressed great satisfaction with the turn-out of all ranks. Weather:- very fine & mild.	68
do	23/1/18	9 am	Barrage Drill. Aircraft Recognition of Target. Gun Drill with Box Respirators. Weather - fine.	
do	24/1/18	9 am	G.S. mechanism, Barrage Drill. Lecture by Commanding Officer to all Officers on Barrage, Shooting under Solid Barrage. Afternoon - Football Weather fine - not cold.	M
do	25/1/18	9 am	Parades by Tactical Scheme - Afternoon Football Inter Section match. Weather - not fine.	M

Army Form C. 2118.

WAR DIARY
or
INTELLIGENCE SUMMARY.
(Erase heading not required.)

Vol 10 Sheet VI

Instructions regarding War Diaries and Intelligence Summaries are contained in F. S. Regs., Part II. and the Staff Manual respectively. Title pages will be prepared in manuscript.

Place	Date	Hour	Summary of Events and Information	Remarks and references to Appendices
MAZIÈRES	26/1/18	9 am	Coy Route March with Lumsden rations to ST. POL returning at 6 PM. Weather - fine but windy	JM
do	27/1/18	9 am	Church Parades in the morning. Kit Inspection by ROs in afternoon. Weather fine	JM
do	28/1/18	9 am	Stables & Transport 9-11 Coy fatigue parade at talks at AMBRINES all men provided with clean underclothing. Lecture by S.O.s on map Reading. LTS EMSLIE & BRYCE proceed on leave to UK. Afternoon Washing limbers. 11 pm Received preliminary orders to move to PENIN. Weather fine	JM
do	29/1/18	9 am	Packing limbers etc preparatory to move, one officer billeting at PENIN. Gun cleaning etc two ORs proceed on leave to UK. Afternoon Inter Section football. Weather fine sharp frost at night	JM
do	30/1/18	9 am	Route March - Unit occupied at 12 noon to move to PENIN at once. Moved to PENIN at 2.20 pm Billeted west of Church. Weather fine - frosty	JM
PENIN	31/1/18	9 am	Section horse SBs Inspection - Gun cleaning - Interesting Amateur Transport two limps etc. Afternoon Football Match with 177th Tng Coy march tied U.2. Weather very cold bright day - fog later	JM

Army Form C. 2118.

ORIGINAL WAR DIARY
or
INTELLIGENCE SUMMARY.
(Erase heading not required.)

VOLUME XI

FEBRUARY, 1918

200TH COMPANY, MACHINE GUN CORPS.

W.C.Mole
Lieut. & Adjt.
for Capt.
COMDG. No. 200 M.G. COY.

Instructions regarding War Diaries and Intelligence Summaries are contained in F. S. Regs., Part II. and the Staff Manual respectively. Title pages will be prepared in manuscript.

Place	Date	Hour	Summary of Events and Information	Remarks and references to Appendices

Army Form C. 2118.

WAR DIARY
or
INTELLIGENCE SUMMARY.
(Erase heading not required.)

VOL II.
SHEET .I.

Place	Date	Hour	Summary of Events and Information	Remarks and references to Appendices
PE NIN	1/2/18	9 am	Combined Drill Centre clearing for prize given by C.O. Platoon awards jointly to "A" + "C" sections. Afternoon Physical Games. Weather fine frosty night	J.W.
do	2/2/18	9 am	Orders received for movement on the 8th inst to the line opposite MERCATEL. Lecture under Section arrangements for reorganization of gun teams. Afternoon Inter section football. Weather fine - cold - misty at night	J.W.
do	3/2/18	9 am	35 men proceeded for the 2nd inn. Church Parade. 2 men proceeded on Construction and Sanitation course. Afternoon - football. Weather Dull misty	J.W.
do	4/2/18	9 am	Inspection of Box respirators - P.H. helmets. Lectures by S.O.S. Afternoon Parade for issue of flat necessaries from Stores. Weather cold misty	J.W.
do	5/2/18	9 am	Route March in full marching order. Afternoon football Weather fine bright	J.W.
do	6/2/18	8 am	Parade for Boots + clean clothing at AMBRINES, cleaning & overhaul of Limbers & transport. Afternoon Inspection of transport by D.A.D.V.S. + O.C. Divl. Train. Weather fine - bright Morn	J.W.
do	7/2/18	6 am	Company moved off march route to COUPEN ARTOIS arriving 3 p.m. Weather Damp misty	J.W.

WAR DIARY or INTELLIGENCE SUMMARY

Army Form C. 2118.

VOL II SHEET IV

Place	Date	Hour	Summary of Events and Information	Remarks and references to Appendices
COOY EN ARTOIS	8/9/18	6 am	Company on move by march route to NEUVILLE VITASSE to arrive 2404.	
			Coy in rear of Battn? Millions, 3 sections in position + in reserve at Coy HQ. Coy HQ at SUGAR FACTORY. Relief complete at 2 p.m. Weather fine bright.	H/M
NEUVILLE VITASSE	9/9/18	9 am	B, C + D Sections in taking positions. A Section in reserve. Work going on improving positions. Observed or relief by 119th Coy M.G.C. on the 10/9/18. O.C. + 2 other officers from 119th Coy arrived at Coy HQ to arrange details of relief. View taken improving gun positions surrounding trenches. Weather fine.	H/M
NEUVILLE VITASSE	10/9/18	9 am	OC rode to DURROW CAMP ahead of Company to arrange accommodation. Two officers proceed ahead also to reconnoitre taking/positions + see the Coy Section officers arrive at 10.30 AM for advance from 119th Coy. 119 Coy arrived at Coy HQ at 12.30 p.m. Relieve of sections complete at 3.30 p.m. "A" Section proceeds to FERVILLERS to take over Batty position. Remaining three sections arrive at DURROW CAMP at 7 p.m. Weather fine night damp.	H/M
DURROW CAMP	11/9/18	9 am	Section officers reconnoitre Batty positions to be occupied in case of emergency except "A" Section which is in position occupied previous day.	

Army Form C. 2118.

WAR DIARY or INTELLIGENCE SUMMARY

Army Form C. 2118.

VOL II SHEET III

Place	Date	Hour	Summary of Events and Information	Remarks and references to Appendices
DURRON P	11/2/18		Night quiet. Sections ordered DPs for gun cleaning. Cleaning of limbers. Transport & 2nd Line moved nearer the camp. C.O. visits Sections & battery position. Weather fine.	
	12/2/18	9 a.m.	Court of Inquiry at HQRs, gun testing. Sections under section officers. Signal xxxx drill. Medical. Two officers proceed to reconnoitre battery positions in reserve line. Weather fine. Section in line nothing to report.	
	13/2/18	9 a.m.	Barrage Drill. Checking of spare parts, ammunition etc. Afternoon into Section football. Weather fine. Section in line nothing to report.	
	14/2/18	9 a.m.	Battles at NOEUX. Section to Nos 1 & 2 by C.O. in his own position. One under C.S.M. Col BRISDEN visit C.O. Section in trench position one casualty (Sligtly) from one of our own batteries. Sergt Mahaffy H.M. proceeds on course of XXXXXXERS. Weather fine. Slight frost at night.	
	15/2/18	9 a.m.	Kit inspection gun drill. Kit into by SOs. 2 officers proceed to LEFT sector to reconnoitre positions. Lts EMSLIE & BRYCE return from leave to U.K. Section in line was bombarded during the night leaving 13 men no casualties. A Private Kit or Shelter occupied by Corporal. Weather fine - sharp cold night.	

WAR DIARY
or
INTELLIGENCE SUMMARY.

Army Form C. 2118.

VOL XI
Sheet 4.

Place	Date	Hour	Summary of Events and Information	Remarks and references to Appendices
DURROW CAMP	16/2/18	9am	Company parade under C.O. 10 Defaulters & 10 M Gunners joined Coy those were posted to 6 Sections. Test of M Gunners by M.O Men. Attended need to elementary gas work under C.S.M. Barrage Drill. Lecture by S.O's subject MG's & the defensive. Afternoon recreation. Weather cold but fine.	WE
do	17/2/18	9am	Church parade in the morning. Warning order received that 3 Sections of Company are to relieve 3 Sections 175 m/g Coy / Section 175 m/g Coy / Section.	WE
do	18/2/18	9am	to front in the line. Weather fine. Company Drill. Barrage Drill & Tactical Scheme in the morning Attached infantry elementary MG training under C.S.M. Cleaning of guns & making preparation for proceeding to the line. Weather fine. Packing of limbers. Kit inspection. Orders issued re relief of 175 m/g Coy. 2nd in command & HQ Coy HQ of 175 m/g Coy 3rd/11th/175 Section arriving at Coy HQ at 3pm "B" Section at 3.20 pm 1st/7 Section at 4pm. relief commenced at 6pm relief complete at 7.55 pm. Transport lines supplied to MOYENN CAMP vacated by 175 m/g Coy transport. 175 m/g Coy took over Coy HQ at DURROW CAMP MORY. Weather very fine.	WE
do	19/2/18	9am		WE

WAR DIARY
or
INTELLIGENCE SUMMARY.

Army Form C. 2118.

Vol VI Sheet 5.

Place	Date	Hour	Summary of Events and Information	Remarks and references to Appendices
ST. LEGER.	20/9/18	11 am	C.O. proceeded to the line & visits all gun positions found everything correct. No wire in command of the Lane & Pontoon. Report from Section officer received at 6.70 am. There was slight hostile artillery activity during the night. Harassing fire was carried out on selected targets. 3000 rounds being fired. Weather very fine.	W.R.
do	21/9/18	4.45pm	Hostile artillery more active than usual especially after dark. Selected targets were fired on by our M.G. 2000 rounds being fired. C.O. visited all positions & found all correct. Coy HQrs 6 to 7 away from the line, held up by W.R under Crushdon. Enemy aircraft attempted to reconnoitre our line but were speedily driven off by our planes. Weather fine but showery.	W.R.
do	22/9/18	5 am	New S.O.S. lines received. These were gone at 6pm & S.O.S. calculations made out & sent to section officers. These were checked by S.O's. Guns laid on new S.O.S. lines by 5.7pm. D.T.G.O. & C.O. visited all gun positions reconnoitred the lines for alternative positions. Enemy very quiet. The usual harassing fire was carried out on selected targets. Weather fine.	W.R.

WAR DIARY
or
INTELLIGENCE SUMMARY

Army Form C. 2118.

VOL XI
Sheet 6.

Place	Date	Hour	Summary of Events and Information	Remarks and references to Appendices
St LEGER	23/7/18	5am	Enemy were active than the day previous. Considerable movement was seen throughout the day. A signalling lamp was observed in the direction of RIENCOURT. The enemy visited for trenches of the divisions on our left about opposite FONTAINE les CROISELLES, N.E. of this locality of coloured lights sent up by that locality the following signal was picked up on the return of their raiding party. Orange flares were sent up from the enemy front line immediately afterwards from both sides. Several rockets went sent up (green & red) these flares were either a signal of shorter range to "Cease fire". Weather very mild. Sent up into the enemy artillery ceased fire.	W.
do	24/7/18		2500 rounds were fired for selected targets	
do	24/7/18	5am	Enemy fairly quiet during the last 24 hours. C.O. visited all gun positions returning at noon. C.O. to Conference 10th Brigade. Harassing fire carried out on selected targets from night firing positions 2000 rounds were fired. Weather fine. Our M.G. fire 2000 rounds on allotted tgts.	W.
do	25/7/18	5am	Hostile artillery more active than usual. Our M.G. fire 2000 rounds on allotted tgts. O.C. visits all positions. Working parties digging in at new battery position. Weather fine wind strong	W.

WAR DIARY or INTELLIGENCE SUMMARY

Army Form C. 2118.

Vol XI Sheet 7

Place	Date	Hour	Summary of Events and Information	Remarks and references to Appendices
ST LEGER	26/9/18	5am	Hostile artillery very active during last 24 hours, 670 of our guns fired in retaliation. SOS were shelled by 4.2s. no damage was done & no casualties. Our MGs fired 3000 rounds on selected targets. O.C. roads given prisoners. At 9.15am the SOS signal went up on the extreme left flank of Div front - WE. In 3 minutes our MGs with lines of our own position fire on front immediately opened fire. Weather fine. Wind fresh	
do	27/9/18	5am	After firing 3100 rounds all was quiet. Weather fine. Wind fresh. Our Aspian bar of our position were shelled with 4.25 several fuse shells. Two aeroplanes were noted for last 4 days in damage & no casualties. An enemy aeroplane came hopped down in No mans land about 11-30 am, 2nd in command went all prisoner. Weather fine. Wind strong	WE
do	28/9/18	5am	Enemy guns active then usual. Our MGs fired 3000 rounds on selected targets. O.C. all gun positions. Keeping eye on enemy no relief in sight. 3/4th by 103 Battery. 9/0 - Bombing forward. Learn to UK. 9/Lt Nuttall & Nutfield. Weather very stormy. Wind strong	WE